大展好書　好書大展
品嘗好書　冠群可期

大展好書　好書大展
品嘗好書　冠群可期

中英文對照武學 8

苗樹林 編著

48式養生
太極拳

附VCD

大展出版社有限公司

四十八式養生太極拳

48 Form Tai Chi for Health Maintenance and Improvement

作者 苗樹林

Writer Shulin Miao

翻譯 崔 婧 孫慧敏

Translator Jing Cui

Huimin Sun

前　言

　　太極拳是我國廣泛流傳的一項歷史悠久、富於民族風格的體育運動。隨著社會的發展及人們需求的變化，原創太極拳的內涵由偏重於技擊性的拳技套路逐漸向以療病、保健、預防早衰和延年益壽爲主的拳術套路發展。這是時代發展的必然結果。太極拳動作的柔和及舒展姿勢，適合生理的不同要求。如果能按照太極拳鍛鍊的規則循序漸進，持之以恆，可增強人體的力量、耐力、速度、靈敏等素質。因此，它適合不同性別、年齡以及從事各種職業的人群，特別是中老年人和體弱者。

　　爲什麼太極拳能延年益壽呢？因爲練太極拳時要求思想高度集中，用意識引導動作，這就調節了大腦的生理功能，使大腦皮層活動強度、靈活性、均衡性得到提高，對外界環境刺激反應的敏感性及調節功能也相應加強，從而使各組織器官能更好地維持正常的生命活動，促進新陳代謝，增強機體免疫和防禦能力，在一定程度上起到防病抗衰的作用。

堅持學練太極拳，能使心肌縮舒力增加，心搏有力，血輸出量增多，進一步增強循環系統的功能，使冠脈血供應充分，保證心臟及全身的血液供應。這樣可預防冠心病、高血壓的發生，使各系統器官的功能得到相應的改善和加強。

學練太極拳，能使呼吸肌功能加強，維持肺組織彈性，改善肺的通氣功能，有利於全身氧氣的供應。

學練太極拳，能促進泌尿系統更好地排泄代謝物，促進內分泌功能，尤其是腎上腺和腎上腺皮質激素分泌，使人體生命更加旺盛。同時，太極拳運動對保持四肢關節及脊柱的靈活性、柔韌性，增加肌肉的力量有明顯的作用。

這套「養身太極拳」叢書，是從多種太極拳派中精選出有益於保健的功架組合而成的。因而學練時，教練者要掌握適當的進度，因人施教；學練者要量力而行，循序漸進。特別是初學者要注意鍛鍊要領，力求姿勢正確，寧可學得慢些，也要做得好些。

Preface

With a long history and national style, Tai Chi is a widely spread martial art in China. Due to the development of the society and popular demand, the focus of Tai Chi has changed from competitions to the treatment of diseases, strengthening health, and prolonging people's lifespan. The soft and stretching Tai Chi movements and postures are more suitable for the physiological needs of human beings. Practicing Tai Chi regularly and consistently will improve one's energy, endurance, speed, and sensitivity. It benefits people of all different ages, genders and vocations, including seniors and the weak.

How does Tai Chi improve the human health? Tai Chi requires the participants to focus their mind and use it to lead the movements, which helps the functions of the cerebrum. It also helps improve the activity, flexibility, and reaction of the cerebral cortex to the environment, which in turn coordinate the tissues and organs more effectively to maintain the normal life activity and to promote the metabolism and the immune system.

Therefore, it helps to achieve the goal of age-resistant and disease-preventing to a certain degree.

Practicing Tai Chi also enhances the cardiac muscles in stretching and contracting to increase cardiac output, and strengthens the function of circulatory system. The coronary artery and the entire body are replenished with blood, effectively reducing the risk of coronary heart disease and hypertension.

Practicing Tai Chi also strengthens the respiratory muscles' function to maintain the elasticity of the lung issue, and helps provide oxygen to the entire body.

Practicing Tai Chi improves the urinary system and promotes the endocrine functions, especially the function of the adrenaline system and adrenal cortical system, in order to gain more vitality.

This sport also plays an important role in increasing flexibility and agility and muscle power in the limbs and the spine.

This series of Tai Chi for Health is comprised of routines that are chosen specifically from various Tai Chi schools, which benefit the health most. Teachers should design different schedules according to individuals. Students should also practice according to their own ability and make progress gradually. At the beginning, one must pay attention to the key points and postures and do his best to follow them correctly.

目　錄

48
式
養
生
太
極
拳

Content

四十八式養生太極拳鍛鍊要領

Key Points to Practice 48 Form Tai Chi for Health Maintenance and Improvement

「養生太極拳」是手、眼、身、法、步協調運動的拳術，並與「吐納術」、「導引術」有機組合，因此，在學練時，首先要瞭解運動的整體性和內外的統一性，即練太極拳時意識、動作、呼吸三者協調進行，做到「一動無有不動」，「一靜無有不靜」。這種運動形式和中國醫學在治療疾病上的整體觀念是一致的。太極拳的指導思想就是要求在練拳時要以意運氣，以意運身，而關鍵在腰。練意、練氣、練身三位一體的鍛鍊方式，構成了太極拳特有的運動規則，也是它能起到保健、療病、增進體質的關鍵所在。

Combined with the skills of Tu Na(Inhale and exhale)and Dao Yin (led by mind), "Tai Chi for Health Maintenance and Improvement" is a routine which coordinates the movements of hands, eyes, body and feet. Therefore, one should first understand the integrity of the movements inside and outside. The mind, the action and the breath should be coordinated with each other

（ "If one part moves, all others follow; if one part stops, all stop" ）. This is the same theory that the Chinese traditional medicine applies in treatment of diseases. The principle of practicing Tai Chi is directing Qi and the body movement with the mind while the waist plays the key role in the process. This approach combines the mind, the breath and the body together to create the unique Tai Chi motion style. It can be used for fitness, curing disease, and strengthening physique.

　　太極拳鍛鍊，始終要保持心平氣和，掌握一個「靜」字，要勢勢做到周身肌肉放鬆，用意識指導動作，保持自然呼吸，動作弧形運轉；漸至做到每個關節和肌肉群都能「一動無有不動」，上下協調，左右連貫，以腰為軸心的運動來帶動四肢百骸的運動，使每一動作均勻連貫，綿綿不斷。上體始終保持不偏不倚，頭頂與尾閭保持上下垂直，避免挺胸、凸肚、低頭、彎腰、弓背、翹臀。目隨手轉，頭頂虛靈，頸鬆而不僵，口微閉，下頜微向內收，舌尖輕抵上齶，肩要鬆垂，肘宜鬆沉，步須虛實。以單腿支撐重心為主，在動作的運轉中保持全身的平衡。隨動作的運轉，用腹自然呼吸，自始至終保持實腹寬胸的狀態，做到上體靈動，下盤穩健，呼吸隨運動漸漸變深、細、勻、緩，促使體力逐漸增強。在每式定式似停非

停的時候，腰要鬆沉下塌，胯根鬆開，用意念使勁力
上到指梢，下到腳尖。目隨手轉，監察四方，意氣，
神氣十足。並隨時保持肩與胯合，肘與膝合，手腳相
應，前後手遙相呼應，上下、左右、前後六部相合，
姿勢圓滿，立身中正，精神飽滿，使整個拳勢形成意
靜、體鬆、勢圓、適勻，功架穩健。

While practicing Tai Chi, one should maintain a peaceful
mind all the time. With the concept of tranquility in mind, relax
the muscle in every movement; use the mind to lead the motion.
Keep a natural breath and move in a curve, gradually achieving the
goal of uniting all the joints and muscles together and coordinate
vertical and horizontal movements. Use the waist as an axle to
lead other parts to move evenly, smoothly and continuously.
Keep the upper body upright, the head and coccyx on a vertical
line. Avoid pushing the chest out, protruding the stomach, bowing
the head, bending waist, arching back or raising the buttocks.
Eyes follow the hands; draw the head upward; relax the neck
without being stiff. Close the mouth lightly with the tip of the
tongue touching the palate lightly, and tuck in the chin slightly.
Relax and sink the shoulders and elbows. Alternate steps between
solid and empty. A single leg supports the weight most the time
and keeps the body balanced during the movements. Breathe
through the abdomen; keep the abdomen strong and the chest

open all the time. Keep the upper body agile and lower body stable. As the breath becomes deeper, slower, thinner and more even, physical strength will be improved. Once a movement comes close to an end, relax and sink the waist, relax the hips; lead the energy up to the fingertips and down to the toes with the mind. Eyes follow the hands and observe around, full of spirit. Keep the shoulders and hips, elbows and knees, hands and feet, and both hands cooperating with each other in six directions: up and down, left and right, front and back. Perfect the postures; stand upright with high spirit and a peaceful mind. Relax the body and move evenly and stably.

　　盤架子的姿勢高低、大小應因人而異，量力而行，不要強行一致。架勢高，動作快，運動量相對較小；而架勢低，動作慢，運動量相對較大。因此，架勢的高低、快慢要根據自身的體質而定。一旦確定架子之後就要始終保持一個水平，不要忽高忽低，忽快忽慢。以健身為目的的練法，要以輕鬆、舒展、自然為總則，以練至微微出汗為度。在開始練習時以高架勢為宜，感到疲勞不支時，可短暫休息後再練，不要勉強練功，更不要以苦練苦熬來追求高功夫，也不要和高技術的練法相比相仿。

Lower the body according to the individual's capability. Do

not push yourself to the same level with others. The high sitting （the degree to which weight-bearing knees are kept bent throughout the form） makes the movement faster and more effortless; low sitting makes the motion slower and requires more effort. Once the height of the posture and speed are set up, one should keep them the same without changing frequently. As the main purpose is fitness, one should practice it in a relaxing, comfortable and natural way; slight perspiration is enough for one session of exercise. At the beginning, it is better to adopt the high sitting stance. Take a rest once tired. Don't force the body into hard work or compare it with other high skill training methods.

一、基本步法

養生太極拳的基本步法有七種，整個套路的運轉變化，都離不開這七種步法的轉換，即虛實之間的相互轉化。從起式以後，要始終僅以一腳支持身體重心，不可犯雙重之弊。因太極拳動作緩慢，因而腿部的負擔量很大，所以初練太極拳時，架子不宜過低，應逐漸降低拳架，來增強腿部的運動量。

1. Basic Step Skills

There are 7 Basic Step Skills in the routine "Tai Chi for Health Maintenance and Improvement". From open to close, every movement is based on the 7 Basic Step Skills. Therefore, every movement bases on shifting the weight from one leg to the other; never move them at the same time. Because Tai Chi movements are slow, the legs have to be strong enough to support the weight. For a beginner, one should start from a little higher, straighter position, and then lower the body gradually to strengthen the legs.

1. 馬 步

馬步要求正身直立，全身放鬆，雙腳分開約兩腳寬度，腳尖向前，落胯下坐。下坐的高低要因人而異，量力而行，但雙膝頭不能超過腳尖。兩膝微向裡扣，鬆肩塌腰，兩肩與雙胯保持上下垂直，眼睛平視正前方，自然呼吸。要實腹、寬胸、圓轉，頭頂百會穴與襠部會陰穴保持上下垂直，成一條直線。兩肩遙遙相對，兩肩之間似有一條線通過。雙手叉腰，兩肘尖遙相對應（圖1-1～圖1-3）。

(1)Horse Step(Ma Bu)

Keep the whole body upright and relaxed. The two feet are about 40–60cm apart, toes pointing forward. Sink the hips and lower the body according to individual ability. Do not bend the knees beyond the toes. Push the knees together slightly. Relax the shoulders and waist. The shoulder and hip of the same side are aligned. Eyes look straight forward. Breathe naturally. The stomach is solid and the chest is open. Keep the Bai Hui (an acupunctural point located on the centre of the top of the head) and Hui Yin (an acupunctural point located on the middle of the crotch) aligned vertically. The shoulders are corresponding as if there is a string connecting them. Place hands on the sides of the waist. The elbows are corresponding (Figure 1–1～Figure 1–3).

2. 丁字步

一腳踏實地面，腳尖向前成斜角，落胯下坐；另一腳前腳掌輕著地面，腳向正前。上體保持正直，兩手輕輕叉腰。目視正前方（圖1-4）。

圖1-1　　　　　圖1-2　　　　　圖1-3

(2)T-Step(Ding Zi Bu)

One foot is planted on the ground, toes pointing forward and out. Sink the hips and lower the body. The front part of the other foot is touching the ground lightly, toes pointing forward. Keep the upper body upright. Put hands on either side of the waist. Eyes look straight forward (Figure 1-4).

3. 弓　步

一腳在前踏實地面，落胯屈膝，腳尖向前，略偏外側，膝蓋不要超過腳尖；另一腳在後，虛踏地面，腳尖微向外偏。上體保持中正。跨步的大小因人而異，不可勉強。兩手叉腰，目視前方（圖1-5）。

(3)Bow Step(Gong Bu)

One foot is planted on the ground, sinking the hip and

圖1-4　　　　　　　　　圖1-5

bending the knee, and the toes pointing forward and a bit outward. The knee should not go beyond the toes. The other foot is
at the back, touching the ground lightly, toes pointing at about
45° outwards in relation to the body. Keep the upper body upright.
Put hands on either side of the waist. Eyes look straight forward
(Figure 1-5).

4. 虛 步

保持弓步姿勢，上身不動，身體重心向後移至後
腳，前腳變為虛步，踏地，腳尖蹺起或不蹺起均可
（圖1-6、圖1-7）。

(4)Empty Step(Xu Bu)

Assume the posture of Bow Step; keep the upper body unchanged. Shift the weight to the back foot, the front foot touching

圖1-6　　　　　　圖1-7

the ground lightly, either with the toes up or on the ground (Figure 1-6, Figure 1-7).

5. 磨轉步

前腳向前橫腳踏地落實，屈膝落胯，塌腰；另一腳向後，腳掌虛點地面，腳跟提起，屈膝，使膝蓋貼近前腿肚（圖1-8）。

(5)Grid Step(Mo Zhuan Bu)

One foot is in the front, planted on the ground, toes pointing inward. Bend the leg, sink the waist and hip. The other foot is at the back, the ball of the foot on the ground lightly. Lift the heel; bend the knee to touch the inner side of the lower leg in the front (Figure 1-8).

6. 仆 步

一腳踏地落實，屈膝，落胯，塌腰，胯部略高於膝蓋（胯與膝平時運動量最大，胯低於膝蓋時其運動量最小），膝蓋不要超過腳尖；另一腳掌向前徐徐橫伸，全腳掌虛貼地面，腿挺直（圖1-9）。

(6)Crouch Stance(Pu Bu)

Plant one foot on the ground, sinking the hip and bending the knee. The hip is a little bit higher than the knee (normally the hips and knees move more and bear more weight during movements – if the hip is lower than the knee, it makes the movement easier）. Do not push the knee beyond the toes. Stretch the other leg forward slowly and place the entire sole on the ground without bending the leg（Figure 1-9）.

7. 獨立步

一腳踏實地面，膝部微屈，腳尖向前，略向外偏斜；另一腳提膝上頂，腳尖微向前下方，腳背部分不要緊張。初練時膝蓋要與臍平，逐漸使膝蓋達到高與心口平。獨立步時須頭部有頂勁領起，氣沉小腹部。落地腳要使腳心含空，用力蹬地，才能站立穩當（圖1-10）。

(7)One Leg Stand(Du Li Bu)

Plant one foot on the ground, bending the knee, toes point-

圖1-8　　　　　　圖1-9　　　　　　圖1-10

ing forward and a bit outward. Lift the other knee with the toes pointing forward and down in a comfortable way. For a beginner, lift the knee up to the navel, later to the chest. Draw the head up. Deliver the Qi to the abdomen. The landing foot needs to have an empty centre and push with force against the ground in order to stand stably (Figure 1-10).

二、步法練習

太極拳講究「邁步如貓行」，「步隨身換」，由腳而腿而腰，須完整一氣，前進後退乃得機得勢。有不得機得勢處身便散亂，必至偏倚，其病必於腰腿求之。虛實宜分清楚，虛非全然無力，實非全然占煞。立身須中正安舒，支撐八面，下部兩腳立根基。這都是練太極拳要注意的步法。步法的邁出要像貓兒行走那樣，既靈敏又穩當，兩腳要保持一虛一實，虛實分明。如果步法不正確，上身姿勢就會東扭西歪，失去平衡，引起局部的緊張，也必然會影響到呼吸的順暢。

2. Step Exercises

Tai Chi requires paying attention to:"taking steps as light as a cat"and "steps follow the body". The feet, legs, and waist move as one. Step forward or backward when time is right. Otherwise, the body will lean, which is caused by the waist and leg going ahead or after the upper body. Distinguish between the substantial and the insubstantial. Insubstantial does not mean completely empty. Substantial does not mean completely tight. Stand comfortably and straight. Feet are planted on the ground as if rooted. It is essential to take alert and stable steps like a cat. One foot is substantial and the other is insubstantial. If the footwork is incorrect, the upper body will lean to one side and lose balance, which will cause parts to tense up and affect the flow of the breath.

怎樣才能練好太極拳的連貫步法呢？在學練太極拳之前，應先練一些太極拳的基本步法。首先，使自己站立穩當，弄清方向路線和腰部的左旋右轉。一些學練太極拳者由於沒有掌握轉動腰部的訣竅，結果大大減弱了太極拳的鍛鍊效果。因此，在學會太極步法的同時，要把腰部的運動掌握好，然後再學練整體動作，這樣就可以大大縮短練習的時間。現介紹一組步法的連貫運動，可參照套路的步法，自行選擇若干組進行練習。

What must be done to make the steps continuous and even? The answer is to start with basic footwork exercises. First, stand steadily and turn the waist to the right or left. Some people do not know the trick in turning the waist, which reduces the efficiency of Tai Chi. Therefore, while one practices the steps, one should also exercise the waist, and then learn the movements and routines. This is the most efficient way. Here are some methods to exercise the waist and steps. Choose some of them to practice.

1. 正身直立，身體重心落在雙腳間，目光向前平視，排除一切雜念，自覺周身放鬆，呼吸順暢，開始動作後用意識不斷地指揮動作（圖1–11）。

（1）Stand straight. The weight is between the feet. Eyes look straight forward. The mind is clear. Relax the whole body, breathe smoothly, and use the mind to lead the motion (Figure 1–11).

圖1–11　　　　　　　　　圖1–12

2. 以意緩緩提起雙手，輕輕叉在腰部（圖1- 12）。

（2）Use the mind to lead the hands to rise. Then place them at either side of the waist（Figure 1-12）.

3. 以意緩緩落胯，屈膝下蹲，成馬步式（圖1- 13）。

（3）Use the mind to lead the waist in sinking down. Bend the knee to a half squat to form a Horse Step（Figure 1-13）.

4. 以意緩緩向右轉腰，使身體重心漸漸移向右腿，頭頸隨著緩緩右轉，目光平視右前方（圖1- 14）。

（4）Turn the waist to the right slowly. Shift the weight to the right leg gradually. The head and neck follow the waist to the right slowly. Eyes look to the right front（Figure 1-14）.

圖1-13　　　　　　　　圖1-14

5. 將身體重心保持在右腿，左腳緩緩收至右腳內側，腳掌虛點地面，左腳尖與右腳跟對齊，相距約一橫腳，成丁虛步（圖1-15）。

(5) Keep the weight on the right leg and move the left foot beside the right foot, the ball of the foot on the ground lightly. Align the left toe with the right heel, 20–30cm apart to form a T-step (Figure 1–15).

6. 腰部緩緩向右擰轉，頭頸也隨著轉動，目光隨之轉向前方平視。同時，左腳跟略提起，向左前方伸出，腳跟著地，膝關節微屈，成虛步式（圖1-16）。

(6) Twist the waist to the right slowly. The head and neck follow the waist to the right. Eyes look straight forward. Meanwhile, lift the left heel a bit, and step to the front left, only

圖1-15　　　　　圖1-16

the heel touching the ground. Bend the knee to form an Empty Step（Figure 1–16）.

7. 身體重心緩緩移至左腿，左腳尖緩緩落地，左腳踏實，後腳虛撐著地，塌腰落胯，成弓步式（圖1–17）。

（7）Switch the weight to the left leg gradually, and put the toes of the left foot onto the ground slowly, then put the entire foot on the ground. Then place the other foot on the ground, sink the waist and hip to form a Bow Step（Figure 1–17）.

8. 身體重心緩緩移至右腳，左腳跟緩緩蹺起，成虛步式（圖1–18）。

（8）Shift the weight to the right foot gradually. Lift the left

圖1-17　　　　　　　　圖1-18

heel to form an Empty Step（Figure 1-18）.

9. 左腳尖向外撇45°，重心緩緩移至左腳，腳橫踩踏實地面；同時，腰部緩緩向左擰轉，右腳跟緩緩提起，腳掌虛點地面順勢磨轉，成磨轉步式（圖1-19）。

（9）Turn the toes of the left foot outward 45°. Shift the weight to the left foot gradually. Place the left foot on the ground, toes pointing inward. Meanwhile, twist the waist to the left slowly. Lift the right heel slowly and grind the ground with the ball of the foot to form a Grind Step（Figure 1-19）.

10. 身體重心仍在左腳，右腳跟緩緩提起，向前落於左腳前側，足掌虛點地面，成丁字步式（圖1- 20）。

（10）Keep the weight on the left foot. Lift the right heel

圖1-19　　　　　圖1-20

slowly and land it in front of the left foot, the ball of the foot on the ground lightly to form a T-Step (Figure 1-20).

三、拳法練習

太極拳的手法包括腕臂的運行，須鬆柔圓活，切忌僵硬呆滯。動作時要旋轉弧形，橫豎順逆均須弧線運轉，使關節圓轉如意，使筋骨組織得到舒鬆。太極拳術語中的「沉肩墜肘」，就是要求把肩關節、肘關節、腕關節放鬆，胸部寬舒，氣不上浮，也利於手臂的伸屈運動，在回縮時力量可略有加大。放鬆肩、肘關節，不是在短時間內可以做到的，必須在每次練拳時用意識引導放鬆。練拳時要用意不用力，用功日久，手臂會產生綿軟曲折的意趣，沉重中帶有輕靈，輕靈中又有沉重之感，輕靈而不飄浮，沉重而不犯僵滯。這就是《太極拳論》中所謂的「勁似鬆非鬆」。

3. Hand Skills

Hand Skills in Tai Chi, including those of the wrist and arm, should be soft, relaxed, round and alert. Do not be sluggish or rigid. Always move in an arc no matter what direction. Turn the knuckles freely and smoothly. Stretch and relax the muscles and bones. Sink the shoulders and elbows, which in Tai Chi mean to relax the joints of shoulders, elbows, and wrists. Open the chest to prevent Qi from floating up, which also helps the arms to extend and increase the force when drawing the arms back. Relaxing the joints in the shoulders and elbows can't be achieved in a short time. One has to pay more attention on daily practice. Led by the mind, and gradually, the arms will feel soft and winding and powerful. That means it is light but not floating, heavy but not stagnant, just as *The Theory for Tai Chi* says: "Relaxation in appearance but powerful inside."

腕關節要圓活，手指宜鬆柔而微屈，前推時要微用掌根著力，而手指則要前探，不要直豎而犯硬，意須貫到指尖。《太極拳論》說：「其根在腳，發於腿，主宰於腰，形於手指」，「勁貫四梢」。四梢即兩腳趾尖、兩手指尖。前輩技擊家都很注重氣血周流全身，勁力集中於指尖的鍛鍊方法。今天我們學練太極拳的目的是為了療病、保健和延年益壽，但仍然要掌握它的鍛鍊原理，發揮它的技擊作用，並體驗它在運動生理上的價值。

Move the joints of the wrist smoothly. Keep the fingers relaxed and bent slightly. When pushing the hands forward, deliver energy to the base of the palms and lean the fingers forward; avoid being upright or stiff. The mind reaches the fingertips. It is described in *The Theory of Tai Chi*: "The feet are roots. The energy is generated from the feet, controlled by the waist, and shown in the fingertips", and "Deliver the energy to the four ends". The ends refer to the toes and the fingertips. All generations of experts in martial arts in the past have paid much attention in practice to circulating the blood and Qi through the whole body and delivering the energy to the fingertips. Today, even though we exercise Tai Chi for the health purpose, it is still necessary to follow the principle, utilize the fundamentals and experience its physiological value.

四、眼法練習

練習太極拳時，眼要隨著主要手的運轉而向前平視。凡動作變化，首先要用意識指導內部（內臟）向預定的方向準備，眼神也要隨之向預定的方向前視，然後身法、步法、手法協調地跟上去，做到意動與形動一致。細心體會，即可逐漸形成意到、眼到、手到，達到練拳時有神有勢。

4. Eye Skills

While practicing Tai Chi, the eyes should follow the leading hand and look directly forward. Before moving, the mind gets the body ready first, and the eyes look toward the next direction. Then the body, the feet and the hands move along coordinately to unify the mind and the action. Experience it carefully, and one can gradually make his movement vigorous and forceful by focusing the mind, eyes and hands.

每式在定勢時，手須做到上對鼻尖，下對腳尖，即拳術中的「三尖相對」。眼須從前手的中指向前平視，意貫指尖，中指的勁到了，其餘四指的勁自然就到了。眼神須照顧上下兩旁，體現出舒展、大方而嚴肅、沉靜的神態。勁只能貫到九分而神氣卻要貫到十分。

Once a movement is settled, the hand, the nose and toes are aligned. This is called "Three Points in Accordance". The eyes must look forward through the middle finger of the front hand, the mind concentrating on the fingertips. As soon as the energy is delivered to the middle finger, it will be in the other fingers as well. The eyes are attentive to the surroundings and the expression is bright, serious and peaceful. While the energy is used up to 90%, the mind must be focused fully at 100%.

五、身法練習

太極拳的身法，是以立身中正，不偏不倚，支撐八面為主。動作不論如何轉換，始終要保持上體的中正，自頭頂軀幹至尾閭要保持上下垂直。前俯後仰，左歪右斜，都違反中正不偏的要求，都屬身法上的缺陷。保持軀幹的中正，對於老年人特別重要。上身前傾是一種衰老的象徵。太極的身法轉換，能做到輕靈圓活，進退穩健，主要靠腰、胯、胸三部的協調運轉，最忌低頭前傾，彎腰弓背。練拳時要始終保持「意守丹田，鬆腰溜臀」，下肢自然就會有穩重之感覺。胸背的肌肉要時時保持鬆舒下沉，自然就會形成「含胸拔背」。含胸拔背不是弓背凹胸，而是將身法的輕靈圓活和沉著穩重相接合，這才是太極拳身法的主要特點。

5. Body Technique

Body Technique in Tai Chi is always centered on keeping the body upright without leaning in any direction. The line connecting the vertex and coccyx is perpendicular to the ground. It is considered as a flaw in body technique if the upper body bends forward or backward or leans right or left. Seniors, especially, should pay more attention to keeping the upper body upright and avoid bending forward. To achieve soft, agile, smooth and stable body movements, the waist, hip and chest must be coordinated with each other. Do not lower the head, lean, bend the waist, or arch the back. Focus the mind on Dan Tian; relax the waist and the hips. The lower limbs stand steadily and naturally. Once the back and chest muscle can be maintained relaxed and sunken, one can naturally "draw in the chest and stretch the back". Do not hollow the chest or arch the back. Combining agility and stability embodies the main features of Body Technique in Tai Chi.

六、呼吸運動

太極拳的呼吸運動採納了「導引術」和「吐納術」的呼吸方法，也就是現在的腹式深呼吸。在盤架走勢中配合呼吸運動，要虛靈頂勁，氣沉丹田。而氣沉丹田的方法是用意識引導呼吸徐徐送入腹部臍下，不使蠻力硬壓；同時，要求立身要中正，全身放鬆。《太極拳論》說：「腹內鬆淨氣騰然」，「氣宜直養而無害」，「內固精神，外示安逸」，都是要求以意運氣，虛靈自然，做到身動、心靜、氣斂、神舒。

6. Breathing Technique

The Breathing Technique in Tai Chi is adopted from "Dao Yin" and "Tu Na" (both are methods to exercise breathing) and is now called "Deep Abdominal Breathing". When coordinating the body movements with breath, draw the head up lightly, and sink the Qi to the Dan Tian. Use the mind to lead the breath slowly down to the lower abdomen without pushing. Meanwhile, the body should be kept upright and relaxed. *The Theory of Tai Chi* says: "When the abdomen relaxes, the Qi flows fluidly"; "The Qi nourishes the body with no harm"; vitality is inside and peace is outside. These are all about using the mind to lead the

Qi gently and naturally, in order to achieve the peaceful mind and breathe naturally and comfortably while the body is moving.

太極拳周身動作比較複雜，初練太極拳時應用自然呼吸法，不可急於採用深呼吸法。練至套路動作熟練後，再配合深呼吸。深呼吸運動也可以單獨訓練，其方法如下：

The body movements in Tai Chi are relatively complicated. At the beginning, it is recommended to breathe naturally rather than deeply. One may breathe deeply once skilled. The deep breath (or abdominal breath) can be trained separately with the following method：

自然站立，身正勢穩，雙腳分開與肩同寬，雙手自然下垂於身體兩側；通體放鬆，頭部虛靈頂勁，目光平視正前方；口唇輕閉，舌抵上齶；排除一切雜念，心平氣和，姿勢穩當。用意念指導雙手向前方緩緩平舉，肘腕微屈，手心向下，以中指領勁上提，同時用鼻緩緩吸氣送入腹下臍部；吸氣將盡，肛門微向上提，使氣聚於臍部，略停，即緩緩以鼻呼氣；肛門放鬆，雙手同時緩緩下按，屈肘內收於腹前。注意按時要以中指領勁輕輕下按，動作和呼吸要緊密配合，協調一致。反覆練習，次數的多少量力而行。

Stand naturally with the body upright. Separate the feet shoulder-width apart. Let the hands naturally hang down at the sides of body. Relax the whole body, draw the head upright and look to the right front directly. Close the mouth lightly with the tip of the tongue touching the roof of the mouth. Get rid of all distracting thoughts and keep the mind in peace and the posture stable. With the mind leading, lift the hands up slowly; bend the elbow slightly with the palm facing downward. While the middle fingers take the lead to rise up, inhale slowly with nose and send the air down to the lower abdomen. When the breath is fully inhaled, tuck the anus in slightly and collect the air at the navel. After a short halt, exhale gently through the nose and relax the anus. Press both hands downward slowly and bend the elbows inward in front of the abdomen. Use the middle fingers to lead the hands to press down. The motion should coordinate with the breath. Repeat above movement according to individual physical ability.

這種以意調息的深呼吸法可使高級中樞神經得到鍛鍊，並可大量吸入氧氣，排出二氧化碳。深呼吸法還可使橫膈腹肌不斷起伏，促進內臟的運動，加強血液循環，因此對各種慢性疾病有一定的治療作用。

This method of abdominal breathing led by the mind can

help activate the central nervous system and may help inhale and exhale a great amount of oxygen and carbon dioxide respectively. It also helps the diaphragm muscle to expand and contract. In addition, it promotes the movement of internal organs and improves blood circulation. Therefore, it possesses the function of treatment of various chronic diseases to a certain degree.

在盤架套路動作熟練以後，可按照起呼落吸、開呼合吸的原則，使呼吸與動作有機地結合起來。但這種深呼吸運動絕不可勉強，一定要做到自然協調，以舒適為度。

After understanding the routine better, one can follow the principle: exhale while rising and inhale while lowering; exhale while opening and inhale while closing to coordinate breathing with movements effectively. One must remember: do not rush to do the Abdominal Breathing, if it does not feel natural or comfortable.

七、勁力運轉

太極拳的動作都是由畫圓走弧線而構成的，也就是說，每一個動作都要有個圓圈。這個圓圈內包含有陰陽兩種勁力，有柔有剛，有虛有實，這是太極拳的特點。

7. Force Delivery

All movements in Tai Chi are made in arches or circles in which there are Yin and Yang, soft and hard, solid and empty. This makes Tai Chi a special style.

太極拳的圓圈運動，有整圓、半圓、順圓、逆圓、直圓和橫圓。它在太極的整體套路內交織變化，動作的前進後退、上起下落、左旋右轉都是弧形運轉的畫圓運動。畫圓走弧線中有斜線、平行線、來復線等多種，符合力學和數學原理。它的內勁運轉像螺旋形的纏繞進退，和中醫的經絡學說有密切的聯繫。

Tai Chi movements can be either complete circles or semi-circles in clockwise, counterclockwise, vertical, or horizontal directions. Switching from one to another makes the routine whole. Whether moving forward or backward, up or down, left or right, always move in circles in which there are oblique, parallel, or duplicated lines, and which conform to the physics and mathematics. Delivering the energy in a spiral, twisted and tangled way is related to the Chinese medical theory of internal energy channels (Those are internal paths to be used for delivering internal power or energy).

初學太極拳時，轉圈走弧線的幅度應以大而圓活為宜，待練習至有體感後則逐漸縮小圓弧幅度。這就是先求開展，後求緊湊的鍛鍊步驟。

For beginners, it is acceptable to move in big, flexible circles. After feeling comfortable with the movements, try to make the circles smaller and smaller. Start in as easy way, then practice it more accurately.

太極拳練到純熟之後，能夠做到一動無有不動，一圈無有不圈，這是由大圈練到小圈，由小圈練至沒圈；由開展漸至緊湊，由有形歸於無跡的最高境界。由極小的圈練到外形上看不出有圈，而只有圈的意思而無圈的形式，這種境界只有功夫極深的專家們才能達到。

When you are skilled in Tai Chi, there are several levels you will reach: when one part of the body moves, all others follow, and circles that reside in circles. Big circles will become small, and small circles will shrink to invisible. The best is to not show the circles, but feeling their presence, which is the highest level that the experts reach.

轉圈動作，不論是大圈、小圈還是沒圈都應依內勁來做統帥，這種內勁是透過前期的鍛鍊，用意識貫注動作而形成的，是似鬆非鬆，似剛非剛，似柔非柔；不剛不柔，亦剛亦柔，剛柔相濟的一種內勁。

Whether the circle is big, small, or invisible, they are all led by internal power, which comes from practicing and focusing the mind on movements. The internal power makes the movements seem soft, but not soft in reality, hard but not hard in reality, and loose, but not that either. The internal power ensures that the movements are not too hard, not too soft, but with elements of both.

內勁的運轉是一種順逆旋轉的纏絲勁，也只有太極拳的圓形運動才能鍛鍊出這種內在的勁力，其他直起直落的拳法是產生不了這種勁力的。

The way to deliver the internal force can be done clockwise or counterclockwise, in a spiral, or twisted or tangled way. Only Tai Chi can generate this kind of force-other martial arts which move in straight lines can never bring out this power.

內勁產生於腹部的丹田。在動作過程中，內勁的運用以上六下四之意識來分配勁力。亦即用意識六分的內勁上行分達兩肩，纏繞轉至兩手指尖端，以四分的內勁下行，經胯分達至兩腿，纏繞運轉至兩腳趾。這種隨動作的開展引伸呼氣而纏繞運轉到四梢時由內而外的順纏，稱為前進纏絲勁。待內勁貫到九分，神

氣貫到十分，姿勢似停非停的時候，動作的開展轉換
為合聚，引伸轉化後回縮，呼氣將盡，轉換後吸氣，
這內勁之上下達四梢之勁力，復由原路線纏繞退回至
腹部（丹田），是由外而內的逆纏，也稱為後退纏絲
勁。

The internal power is generated from the Dan Tian (Abdomen). When in use, 60% of the power goes up to the shoulders, twisting to the tips of the fingers. 40% moves down through the hips to legs, twisting to the toes. The way to deliver the force externally and twist it to the end of the body with movement and breathing is called Twisted Force Forward. When the force reaches 90%, the spirit reaches 100%. Right before the postures are finished, gather the power, and breathe deeply. The power goes backward to the stomach; this is called Twisted Force Backward.

上述纏繞進退的纏絲勁練法是完全符合中醫經絡
學說的，它對調和氣血，增強體質極有成效，而在技
擊技法上的應用也是必修的內容，過去的太極拳家將
此當作不傳之秘。

Delivering the internal power in a twisted and tangled way helps to adjust the Qi and blood flow and improves physical status. It is also essential in improving Tai Chi skills, which is trained by some experts as a secret.

關於內勁運轉時的輕重、剛柔、虛實，應該是或隱或現，需要學練者專心揣摩，細心體會，靈活運用。每式的起承轉合著著貫穿、節節放鬆、處處合住的鍛鍊方法，不但要細心揣摩，而且要多看，多請教有經驗的老師指導示範，才能有較快的進步。

Delivering the internal power in soft or hard, solid or empty, light or heavy, apparent or hidden ways requires concentration and paying attention to feeling during practice or use. Switch one movement to another continually, easily, and coordinately. You will make good progress in watching skilled people and taking advice from experienced teachers often.

八、太極拳與經絡學說

太極拳是以陰陽學說為理論基礎的。《太極拳論》說：「太極者，無極而生，動靜之機，陰陽之母也。」它的動作柔和，圓活連貫，均勻協調，完全有利於人體氣血的流暢。太極拳鍛鍊的理論指導思想是：以意運氣，運勁如抽絲，運勁如九曲珠無微不至。立身中正安舒，不偏不倚，無過無不及等理論原則，都和經絡學說有著密切的關係。經絡學說是我國當代醫學家經過歷代長期的研究、觀察、實踐逐步發展起來的一種解釋生理和病理的學說，而太極拳的創編正是建立在經絡學說的宏觀基礎上。太極拳的動靜、開合、虛實、剛柔以及以意運氣、以氣運身的螺旋形運行內勁、纏絲勁練法，完全是根據我國古代的經絡學說而創編的。近百年來太極拳運動的開展，對防病、治病、保健作出了重要貢獻，這是不可否認的事實。

8. Tai Chi and the Chinese Medical Theory of Channels

The foundation of Tai Chi is Yin and Yang. *The Theory of Tai Chi* says that "Tai Chi" means the state beyond the limit, to alternate between stillness and movement at the right time, and that it is the source of Yin and Yang. Tai Chi movements are gentle, comfortable, flexible, continuous, even, and coordinative, which benefit the blood activity and energy flow. The principle of Tai Chi exercises are based on using the mind to lead Qi (internal energy), and using force as if drawing on a thread. The movements are like beads on a string, all linked. Keep the body upright without leaning in any direction. Push the limits without over stressed. All of these are related to the theory of channels (An internal system to carry energy), which was created by medical scientists through study, observation and practice to explain physiological and pathological phenomena. Tai Chi's movement or rest, the open or close, the insubstantial or substantial, soft or hard all based on the theory. Always use the mind to lead Qi; use Qi to lead the body and deliver the internal power in a twisted and tangled way. For almost one hundred years, Tai Chi has contributed significantly to the prevention and treatment of diseases, which is an undeniable fact.

四十八式養生太極拳動作名稱

List of the Movement of 48 Form Tai Chi for Health Maintenance and Improvement

預備式

一、靜立導引

二、吐故納新

三、啟動真元

四、白鶴亮翅

五、摟膝拗步

六、右攬雀尾

七、單鞭勢

八、左手揮琵琶

九、挒擠三勢

十、左搬攔捶

十一、左攬雀尾

十二、十字手

十三、斜身靠

十四、肘底捶

十五、倒攆猴

48
式
養
生
太
極
拳

Preparing

1. Stand Still with Mind Concentrated

2. Get Rid of the Stale and Take in the Fresh

3. Start

4· White Crane Spreading Wings

5. Brush Knee and Twist Steps

6. Grasping Bird's Tail – Right

7. Single Whip

8. Playing a Pipa (Chinese Lute) – Left

9. Pulling and Pushing

10. Deflect, Parry and Punch – Left

11. Grasping Bird's Tail – Left

12. Cross Hands

13. Lean the Body and Push with the Shoulder

14. Fist under the Elbow

15. Step Backward and Push

16. Push Diagonally

17. Playing a Pipa (Chinese Lute) – Right

18. Step up, Pull and Push

19. Step up and Punch

20. Snake Turns and Puts out his Tongue

21. Pat the Foot and Catch a Tiger – Left and Right

22. Throw the Left Fist

四十八式養生太極拳動作名稱

23. Thrust the Fist and Lower Body

24. Lift the Hand and Stand on One Leg – Left and Right

25. Step Back to Pull the Bird's Tail

26. Single Whip

27. Cloud Hands – Right

28. Splitting Wild Horse's Mane

29. Patting a High Horse

30. Kicking with the Right Heel

31. Striking Ears with Both Fists

32. Kicking with the Left Heel

33. Hidden Punch

34. Neddle to the Sea Bottom

35. Flashing the Arm

36. Separate Feet

37. One Hand Blocks and the Another Strikes

38. Step Forward and Grasp the Enemy

39. As if Blocking and Shutting

40. Left Cloud Hand

41. Throw the Right Fist

42. Working with a Shuttle

43. Step Backward and Thrust the Hand

44. Push Down in Empty Step

45. Stand on One Leg to Lift the Hand

48
式
養
生
太
極
拳

46. Push with the Shoulder

47. Turn and Lower the Body While Pulling Hand

48. Step forward and Cross the Fists

49. Closing

四十八式養生太極拳圖解說明

Detailed Explanation of 48 Form Tai Chi for Health Maintenance and Improvement with Drawings

預備式

　　自然站立，兩腳併攏，頭頸正直，胸腹放鬆，肩背鬆垂，下頜內收，兩臂輕貼兩大腿外側。精神集中，眼向前平視，呼吸自然。左腳輕輕向左分開半步與肩同寬，腳尖向前（圖3-1、圖3-2）。

圖3-1　　　　　　　　　　　圖3-2

Preparing

Stand naturally, feet together, head upright. Relax the chest, stomach, shoulders, and back. Tuck in the chin. Both arms hang down by the sides of the thighs. The mind focuses. Eyes look forward; breathe naturally. The left foot takes a half step to the left. The two feet are shoulders' width apart, toes pointing forward (Figure 3-1, Figure 3-2).

一、靜立導引

正面導引：按圖3-3程序用意念體察一遍。
背面導引：按圖3-4程序用意念體察一遍。
臂手導引：按圖3-5程序用意念體察一遍。

1. Stand Still with Mind Concentrated

Front is as Figure 3-3。

Facial 面部
Throat 喉部
Chest 胸部
Abdomen 腹部
Lower Abdomen 小腹部
Perineum 會陰部

圖3-3

Back is as Figure 3–4。

Hand and Arm are as Figure 3–5。

二、吐故納新

【訣要】

> 納新吐故意須圓，攝得眞精頂內前；
> 提神貫頂精神注，坐腕沉肘勢自然；
> 納氣兩手往上行，起在丹田升在胸；
> 腹內精氣全提住，勢若騰空上蒼穹；
> 待得吸盡變成吐，清氣沉來濁氣除；
> 腹鬆手按歸原位，渾然一身還太靈；
> 六字眞訣配呼吸，呵噫呼嘘吹與呬；
> 二氣循環無上下，演成36個小周天。

圖3-4　　　　圖3-5

48
式
養
生
太
極
拳

2. Get Rid of the Stale and Take in the Fresh

Highlight

Inhale and exhale with a focused mind.

Hold the body as one.

Fill with energy, alert and ready to start.

Sink the wrists and elbows naturally.

Inhale as hands move up.

The Qi rises from the abdomen to the Chest.

Exhale to get rid of stale air.

Relax the abdomen as hands push down.

Go back to the original position, at ease.

Feel light and fresh,

Make six sounds along the breathing:

Ha, Yi, Hu, Xu, Chui and Si.

Repeat the inhaling and the exhaling

to finish 36 Small Zhou Tian Exercises.

Note: the cycle between Ren channel and Du channel called the Small Zhou Tian.

36 Small Zhou Tian is a method to exercise Ren channel (An internal energy channel along the spine) and Du channel (An internal energy channel along the middle line of the front of the

body). Look at the (6) for detail.

1. 緊接上式，兩手五指伸展，兩臂同時向外擰轉，掌心向後，掌指向下（圖3-6）。

(1) Extend the fingers. Twist both arms outward, palms facing back, fingers pointing down (Figure 3-6).

2. 兩掌同時坐腕，掌心向下，掌指向前（圖3-7）。

(2) Sink both wrists so that palms face down, fingers pointing forward (Figure 3-7).

3. 兩掌同時向外轉掌，掌指向兩側，掌心仍然向下（圖3-8）。

(3) Turn both hands outward, palms facing down, fingers

圖3-6　　　　圖3-7　　　　圖3-8

pointing out（Figure 3-8）.

4. 兩掌同時由身體兩側向小腹前向上畫弧抱起，掌心向上，兩掌五指相對，置於臍下小腹前，兩肘微屈成捧球狀（圖3-9）。

（4）Move hands from either sides of the body to the navel, palms facing up, and the fingers of one hand pointing at the fingers of the other hand. Bend the elbows slightly as if carrying a ball（Figure 3-9）.

5. 兩掌不停，繼續由小腹沿腹部中線向上抬至兩乳。同時，用鼻緩緩吸氣，提肛縮便，小腹內收（圖3-10）。

（5）Continue to move both hands upward along the middle

圖3-9　　　　　　　　圖3-10

line of the body to the chest. Inhale through the nose; tuck in the anus and stomach（Figure 3–10）.

6. 稍停，兩掌向內翻掌，掌心向下，雙手五指仍然相對，向下按至臍下小腹前；同時，用嘴吐「呵」字訣呼氣（圖3-11a、圖3-11b）。如上動作反覆做六次起落，為「呵」字歌訣的第一循環。第二至第六循環與第一循環程序相同，唯在吐氣時之訣分別為噫、呼、噓、吹、呬。每個循環均為六起六落，六呼六吸，每一循環用一個音訣，總共為36次呼吸，為演成36個小周天。

（6）Pause a little while; turn both hands inward so the palms are facing down, the fingers of one hand pointing at the fingers of the other hand. Push both hands down under the navel. Meanwhile, exhale with sound "Ha"（Figure 3–11a, Figure 3–

圖3-11a　　　　　　圖3-11b

11b). Repeat the above movement 6 times. Then with each sound of "Yi, Hu, Xu, Chui, Si", repeat the above movement 6 times. Therefore, 6×6=36 in total to make 36 Small Zhou Tian Exercises.

三、啟動眞元

1. 接上式，雙掌由腹前向下自然垂落於身體兩側，掌心向內，五指向下，中指不動，餘指緩緩向前後分開，要儘量張足，使掌心成凹形（圖3-12）。

3. Start

（1）Move the hands naturally downward past the abdomen to the sides of the body, palm facing inward and fingers pointing down. While keeping the middle finger unchanged, stretch the other fingers as far apart as possible. Palms are concave (Figure 3-12).

圖3-12

2. 肘尖略向外撐，以整個臂帶動肘、腕向外轉臂，手掌心隨之向後（圖3-13）。

（2）Push the elbow slightly outward. The arms lead the elbows and wrists turning outward, palms facing back accordingly (Figure 3-13).

3. 雙掌向前上方翹指，掌心隨之向下，五指仍張足，雙臂伸直，身體直（圖3-14）。

（3）Tilt the fingers until the palms face down. Keep the fingers apart. Extend the arms and stand straight（Figure 3-14）.

4. 雙腕向外側擰旋，上臂微微靠攏身體。同時，以小指領先向後擰轉，五指併攏，掌心仍向下，五指向後（圖3-15）。

圖3-13　　　　　圖3-14　　　　　圖3-15

（4）Twist both wrists outward, and bring the upper arms slightly close to the body. Meanwhile, the little fingers take the lead and twist backwards; draw the fingers together and point them backward, palms facing down (Figure 3–15).

5. 先將拇指扣回一節，然後屈肘，上臂保持不動，用掌根緩緩向前上提至與肩平，掌心朝天，手指朝前。同時，雙膝微屈（圖3–16a、圖3–16b）。

（5）Bend the thumbs and the elbows. Keep the upper arms unchanged and raise both bases of the palms slowly upward to shoulder level, palms facing up and the fingers pointing forward. At the same time, bend the knees slightly (Figure 3–16a, Figure 3–16b).

圖3–16a   圖3–16b

6. 先展開拇指，雙掌以拋物線角度向前上方穿出，力在雙手指腹，穿掌要具彈力，手心向天（圖3-17a、圖3-17b）。

(6) Extend the thumbs. Thrust the palms towards the upper front along a curve of a parabola with the force on the first knuckles of the fingers, palms facing up (Figure 3-17a, Figure 3-17b).

7. 雙肘下沉在胸前，兩肘尖儘量呈「V」字形靠攏，手心朝天，手指朝前（圖3-18）。

(7) Sink the elbows and draw them together in front of the chest to form a "V" shape, palms facing up and the fingers pointing forward (Figure 3-18).

圖3-17a　　　　圖3-17b　　　　圖3-18

8. 雙肘向左右兩側展開，兩手掌隨勢成立掌相對，掌指向上，兩掌相距約一拳之寬（圖3-19）。

(8) Move the elbows outward to the opposite sides of body and raise the palms to face each other with a distance of a fist between them, fingers pointing up (Figure 3-19).

9. 立掌擴胸。擴胸時兩掌先向內合，兩肘尖再向左右略朝外撐，兩掌保持立掌相對（圖3-20）。

(9) While stretching the chest, first move the palms close to each other and pull the elbows slightly outward. Both hands remain upright and facing each other (Figure 3-20).

10. 鬆肩合掌。先鬆開雙肩，兩手從左右兩側向胸前合掌，四指併攏，指尖朝天，雙拇指指尖指向膻中

圖3-19　　　　　　圖3-20

穴；同時，將合攏之掌略向胸前推出，拇指尖與膻中
穴相距約兩寸（圖3-21）。

(10) Relax the shoulders and put the palms together in
front of the chest with the fingers close together and pointing
upward, the tips of the thumbs pointing to the "Shan Zhong
Xue" (An acupuncture point at the middle of the stomach).
Meanwhile, push the palms slightly up to the chest with the
tips of the thumbs 7cm away from the "Shan Zhong Xue" (An
acupuncture point at the middle of the chest) (Figure 3-21).

11. 收腹下行。先屈膝下蹲，再收腹，隨後將合攏
的雙掌緩緩下移；當下移到雙掌不能再相合時，隨下
移之勢兩掌逐漸分開（圖3-22）。

(11) Bend the knees and lower the body. Draw in the ab-

圖3-21   圖3-22

domen and move the palms down slowly. Separate the palms gradually (Figure 3–22).

12. 分掌下按。當下移雙掌至臍平時，兩掌在臍部向左右兩側分開；同時，下腹鼓起，分開的雙掌要保持雙手中指相對，中指之間相距約三寸（圖3–23）。

(12) Move the palms down to navel level. At the same time, bulge the lower abdomen. The middle fingers point at each other with a distance of about 10cm between them (Figure 3–23).

四、白鶴亮翅

【訣要】

兩臂環擊狀似門，閑來無事練撲勁；
白鶴展翅稱雄後，顧盼輕靈任自行；
步要丁虛勢要蹲，即行即擊快如風；
腰輪平轉脊須正，舒展雙翅敵難封。

4. White Crane Spreading Wings

Highlight

Stretch the arms in an arc as if opening a door.

Practice eagle diving and rushing.

Look and move neatly and freely with an eagle's force.

Lower the body in a T–step and an Empty Step,

ready for movement as fast as wind.

Turn the waist steadily and keep the back straight.

Spread arms forcefully, defended against by no one.

1. 接上式，兩掌向兩側平分開，掌心向下，手指向前，屈肘，沉肩，勢下蹲（圖3-24a、圖3-24b）。

（1）Move the hands to the opposite sides levelly, palms facing down, fingers pointing forward. Sink the shoulders and elbows. Lower the body（Figure 3-24a, Figure 3-24b）.

2. 上體微向左擰轉，身體重心移向左腿。左掌微上提，左臂屈收在左胸前，右手經腹前向左畫弧，兩掌左上右下，掌心相對，在左胸前成抱球狀。同時，右腳提起隨即內收，眼看左手前方（圖3-25）。

圖3-23　　　　圖3-24a　　　　圖3-24b

（2）Slightly turn the upper body to the left. Shift the weight onto the left leg. Slightly raise the left palm and bend the elbow in front of the chest to the left. Draw the right hand in an arc to the left before the abdomen. The left hand is above the right hand, palms facing to each other as if holding a ball. Meanwhile, lift the right foot and draw it in, eyes looking to the left front（Figure 3–25）.

3. 右腳向右後撤半步，身體重心隨即移於右腿，腰隨之向右側擰轉。右掌自左下方向右上方畫弧，左掌經右肩前向下畫弧。眼看右掌（圖3-26）。

（3）The right foot takes a half step to the back right. Accordingly shift the weight onto the right leg. Twist the waist to the right. While the right palm draws an arc from the lower left to the upper right, the left palm passes the right shoulder and draws an arc

圖3-25　　　　圖3-26　　　　圖3-27

downward. Eyes look at the right palm (Figure 3–26).

4. 上體微向左擰轉，面向正前方。兩掌繼續向相反方向畫弧，左掌按於左胯旁，掌心向下，指尖向前；右掌提至額前右上方，掌心向內，兩臂均保持弧形狀。同時，左腳稍向右腳內移，腳掌點地，雙膝微屈，成左虛步。眼平視前方（圖3-27）。

(4) Turn the upper body to the left slightly to face the front. Draw two hands in arcs in opposite directions. Press the left hand down by the left hip, palm facing down, fingers pointing forward. Raise the right palm to the upper right in front of the forehead, palm facing inward. Both arms are arched. At the same time, move the left foot close to the right foot with the ball of the foot on the ground, and both knees bend slightly to form a left Empty Step. Eyes look forward (Figure 3–27).

【要點】

虛步時，兩腳夾角大約為45°，後腿膝蓋與腳尖，臀部與腳跟上下相對，上體保持正直，要縮胯收臀，雙膝部均須向前。

Key Points

When making the Empty Step, the feet form a 45° angle. The knee of the back leg aligns with the toes, and the same for the hip and the heel. Keep the upper body upright. Pull the hips and buttocks in, both knees pointing forward.

五、摟膝拗步

【訣要】

起肩過胯膝外摟，指點掌印蓋當頭；

眉間一聲霹靂震，小丑天魔亦罷休；

肘處須防敵暗推，連環摟打任施為；

任他強硬如山岳，肩頭一掌或鳩尾。

5. Brush Knee and Twist Steps

Highlight

Move a hand from the shoulder,

by the hip, around the knee and then over the head.

Move another hand to attack the enemy's forehead;

even devils are scared away.

Protect yourself with the elbows and attack continuously.

No matter how strong an opponent is,

he will be beaten by the strike on his shoulder or tailbone.

1. 接上式，上體微向左擰轉，右掌經體前畫弧下落，左掌經體側畫弧上舉（圖3-28）。

（1）Turn the upper body to the left slightly. Draw the

right hand in an arc downward in front of the body. Raise the left hand to draw an arc along the side of body（Figure 3–28）.

2. 上體向右擰轉，右掌經下向右後上方畫弧至與耳同高，掌心斜向上；左掌同時經面前向右下畫弧至右胸前，掌心斜向下。同時，左腳收至右腳內側。目視右掌（圖3–29）。

（2）Turn the upper body to the right. The right hand draws an arc toward the upper right back and stops at the level of the ear, palm facing diagonally up. The left hand moves in front of the face to draw an arc toward the lower right and stops in front of the right chest, palm facing diagonally down. Meanwhile, move the left foot close to the right foot. Eyes look at the right hand（Figure 3–29）.

圖3–28　　　　　圖3–29

3.上體微向左擰轉，左腳向偏左前方邁出一步，身體重心向前移動，左膝前屈，右腿自然伸直，成左弓步。同時，右掌屈收經右耳側向前推出，指尖向上高於鼻尖，左掌向左下經左膝前方摟過，按於左胯側，掌心向下，掌指向前。保持上體正直，鬆腰鬆胯，目視右掌（圖3-30）。

（3）Turn the upper body to the left. The left foot takes a step to the left front. Shift the weight forward. Bend the left knee and extend the right leg naturally straight to form a left Bow Step. At the same time, draw back the right palm and push it forward from the right ear, fingers pointing up at a level higher than the nose. The left hand brushes over the left knee while moving toward the left back. It pushes down by the left hip, the palm facing down and fingers pointing forward. Keep

圖3-30

the upper body upright; relax the waist and hips. Eyes look at the right palm (Figure 3–30).

【要點】

形成弓步時，兩腳夾角為45°～60°，左膝和左腳尖上下垂直，兩腳不要踩在前後一條直線上，以保持身體重心穩定；更不能左右腳交叉。根據上體扭轉程度和勁力方向，兩腳須保持橫向10～30公分的距離。

Key Points

In the Bow Step, the feet form an angle of 45–60°. Keep the left knee and toes vertically aligned. In order to keep the weight stable, do not place both feet on the same line; do not cross the feet either. According to the power and the direction of the body turn, keep the feet 10–30cm apart.

六、右攬雀尾

【訣要】

混沌初開日，陰陽一倒看；
掤按像乾坤，捋擠似離坎；
掤勁含剛健，乘龍欲上天；
按順坤柔往，從人自不難；
捋是剛中柔，顧後更防前；
擠如柔中剛，發勁莫遲緩；

知此四正方，不外太極圈。

6. Grasping Bird's Tail – Right

Highlight

Push and press forcefully.

Draw and pull gently but strong.

Defend both front and back.

Attack quickly and without hesitation.

1. 接上式，上體後坐，身體重心移至右腿，左腳尖向上蹺起，並微向內扣，上體隨之向右擰轉。右臂隨轉體向下帶至胸平，右掌掌心向上，左掌自左下方經體側向體前畫弧，高與肩平，掌心斜向下。頭隨體轉動，目視前方（圖3-31）。

(1) Move the upper body backward. Shift the weight onto the right leg. Raise the toes of the left foot up and turn them inward slightly. Turn the upper body to the right accordingly and move the right arm backward to the level of the chest, palm facing up. Move the left hand from the lower left to draw an arc forward along the body to the shoulder level, palm facing diagonally down. The head follows the body and turns; eyes look forward (Figure 3-31).

2. 左腳落地，身體重心移至左腿，右腳收至左腳內側。同時，左前臂微微回收，右臂外旋，右掌心向上，從左肘下方向右前方穿出（圖3-32）。

（2）Place the left foot on the ground. Shift the weight onto the left leg. Move the right foot close to the left foot. Meanwhile, slightly draw back the left forearm. Rotate the right arm outward, palm facing up, and thrust the hand under the left elbow to the upper right（Figure 3-32）.

3. 右腳向右前方邁出一步，身體重心向前移至右腿，右腿前屈成右弓步。同時，左掌附於右腕內側，兩掌同時自左向前推出，由下至上走弧形，右掌心向內，左掌心向外（圖3-33）。

（3）The right foot takes a step to the right front. Shift the

圖3-31   圖3-32

weight to the right leg. Bend the right knee forward form a right Bow Step. Meanwhile, attaching the left palm to the right wrist, push both hands from the left to draw an arc forward and upward, the right palm facing inward and the left palm facing outward (Figure 3-33).

4. 上式不停，上體後坐，右腳尖上蹺。右掌自前向右、向後屈肘再畫半個平圓，右掌心斜向內，左掌心斜向外。上體轉向正前方，鬆腰鬆胯，眼看正前方（圖3-34）。

(4) Shift the upper body backward, and raise the toes of the right foot up. Bend the elbow and move the right palm in a flat semicircle towards the right back. The right palm faces diagonally inward and the left palm faces diagonally outward. Turn the upper

圖3-33　　　　　　圖3-34

body to the front and relax the waist and hips. Eyes look to the front (Figure 3-34).

七、單鞭勢

【訣要】

單鞭一勢最稱雄，左像箭來右似弓；

鬆肩沉肘擋四面，鋼鞭一擊迫人魂；

近得身來便是捌，或推或按任君施；

左顧右盼迎頭打，先擊敵人兩枝花。

7. Single Whip

Highlight

This posture makes you a true hero,

an arrow from the left, and a bow on the right.

Relax the shoulders and elbows to defend

and attack in all directions.

Strike powerfully as if holding a steel whip and scare the soul.

Pull, push or block when he comes close.

Beat directly; strike two birds with one stone.

But do not forget precaution.

1. 接上式，右腳內扣落實，上體微向左轉，重心移向右腿，左腳隨之收於右腳內側。同時，右前臂在右肩前內旋後畫弧前伸，右掌隨之前按，至右前方時右掌變勾手；左掌亦隨右掌一起翻轉，收停於右肘內側，掌心向內。眼看右手（圖3-35）。

(1) Turn the right foot inward and place it on the ground solidly. Slightly turn the upper body to the left. Shift the weight onto the right leg, and draw back the left foot close to the right foot. Meanwhile, the right forearm rotates inward before the right shoulder and then draws an arc forward; the right palm accordingly pushes forward and turns into a hook (by putting all the fingers and thumb together) as it reaches the right front. The left hand follows the right hand and turns over at the same time, then stops by the inner side of the right elbow and facing inward. Eyes look to the right hand (Figure 3-35).

2. 上體微向左轉，左腳向左前方邁出一步，身體重心左移成左弓步。同時，上體繼續左轉，左前臂內旋，左掌慢慢向前推出，掌心向前，指尖向上高與鼻平，左手左腳上下相對。眼看左掌（圖3-36）。

(2) Turn the upper body slightly to the left. The left foot takes a step toward the left front. Shift the weight onto the left leg to form a left Bow Step. Meanwhile, continue to turn the body to the left. Rotate the left forearm inward, and push the palm forward slowly at nose level, palm facing forward, fingertips

pointing up. The left hand and left leg are aligned vertically. Eyes look to the left hand（Figure 3–36）.

【要點】

推掌按掌以後手臂要稍屈，肘要鬆沉，不可僵直或聳肩揚肘。初學者在收腳上步時，前腳掌可在支撐腳內側輕輕點地，以利重心穩定；重心前移成弓步時，後腿自然蹬直，膝部不要僵挺，腳跟可以隨後展調整。

Key Points

After pushing or pressing, bend the arms slightly and relax the elbows. Do not be rigid or raise the shoulders or the elbows. For beginners, when withdrawing the foot and stepping forward, the ball of the front foot can lightly touch the ground in order

圖3-35　　　　圖3-36

for the weight to remain stable. When shifting the weight forward to form a Bow Step, extend the back leg naturally straight and adjust the heel accordingly.

八、左手揮琵琶

【訣要】

雙手緊抱一琵琶，拆幹剪腕用不差；

裏外圈兒由我畫，揮擊專會破擒拿；

上打玄關下打陰，中間便是虎掏心；

此種機關休洩露，一著傷人禍不輕。

8. Playing a Pipa(Chinese Lute) – Left

Highlight

Two hands are corresponding as if holding a Pipa,

the purpose of which is to bend the enemy's body or wrist.

Draw circles with both hands and avoid being caught.

Use this movement to strike on his head, crotch, or heart.

Do not use it rashly in case of injuring a person

and creating more conflict.

1. 接上式，左腳支撐重心，腹部鬆縮，上體微向左擰轉；右腳提起跟進半步，腳前掌著地，落在左腳後面。同時，左掌向內、向下畫弧至左胯前，右勾手變掌，隨腰的轉動向內、向前平擺至體前，掌心斜向上。眼看前方（圖3-37）。

（1）The left foot supports the weight. Relax the abdomen and draw it in slightly. Turn the body slightly to the left. Lift the right foot and place it after the left, the ball of the foot on the ground. Meanwhile, move the left palm inward and downward to draw an arc to the left hip. Change the right hand back into an open palm and, following the turn of the waist, move it inward and forward in front of the body, palm facing diagonally up. Eyes look to the front (Figure 3-37).

2. 身體重心向後移動，右腳落實，左腳向前稍上步，腳跟著地，膝微屈，成左虛步。同時，右掌隨腰部微向右擰轉，屈肘回帶，掌心轉向下，左掌向外、

圖3-37　　　　　　　圖3-38

向前上方畫弧挑舉。然後兩臂鬆沉含勁，左掌成側立掌停於面前，指尖與眉心相對；右掌也成側掌，屈臂合於胸前，掌心與左肘相對。眼看左掌（圖3-38）。

(2) Shift the weight backward. Place the right foot on the ground firmly. The left foot takes a small step forward, the heel touching the ground, knee bent to form a left Empty Step. At the same time, the right palm follows the waist and bends to draw back the hand, palm facing down. Move the left palm outward and forward in an arc. Then relax and sink the arms to accumulate power. The left hand stands up in front of the face, fingers pointing up at the middle of the eyebrows. Bend the right arm in front of chest. The right hand stands up too, facing the left elbow. Eyes look to the left palm (Figure 3-38).

【要點】

右腳落地時先以前腳掌著地，隨著重心後移之勢，再慢慢全腳掌踏實地面；提步時，腳跟先離地，然後輕輕將全腳提起。提步、落步要用力輕而勻，不可突然蹬地、砸地。

Key Points

When placing the right foot on the ground, put the ball of the foot on the ground first, and shift the weight backward, then slowly place the entire foot on the ground solidly. When lifting the foot up, lift the heel off the ground first and then lift the entire foot up lightly. Use the force evenly and gently. Do not push the ground abruptly or step on the ground heavily.

九、捋擠三勢

【訣要】

順其來勢攻，導之使長延；
輕靈不丟頂，力盡自然空；
重心需自持，莫被他人乘；
此為捋勁意，引近我身邊。
直接單純意，迎合一動中；
間接反應力，如球撞壁還；
又如錢投鼓，咚咚聲鏗然；
此為擠勁意，用時有兩方。

9. Pulling and Pushing

Highlight

Let the enemy get close;

pull him in the same direction of his attach;

lead him further.

Pull and ready to push at any time;

keep yourself stable.

Do not give him a chance.

Push when he tries to escape;

use his own force to attack him like a ball rebounding

from a wall or a coin on the drum:

quickly and forcefully.

1. 緊接上式，左腳稍向左外挪動，然後全腳落實，重心前移成左弓步。上體稍右轉，右掌自左前臂上穿出，由左向右前方畫弧平抹，掌心斜向下；左掌微外旋，掌心斜向上並向後畫弧，收至右肘內側下方。眼看右掌（圖3-39、圖3-40）。

（1）Move the left foot slightly outward to the left and place the entire foot solidly on the ground. Shift the weight forward to form a left Bow Step. Turn the upper body slightly to the right. Thrust the right palm over the left forearm and draw an arc levelly

圖3-39　　　圖3-40　　　圖3-41

from left to the right front, palm facing diagonally down. Move the left palm slightly outward and backward in an arc, and stop it under the right elbow, palm facing diagonally up. Eyes look to the right palm (Figure 3-39, Figure 3-40).

2. 兩掌自前向下捋，左掌捋至左胯外側，右掌捋至腹前。同時，右腳收於左腳內側。眼看右前方（圖3-41）。

(2) Pull the arms downward in front of the body, and stop when the left palm by the outside of the left hip and the right palm before the abdomen. Meanwhile, move the right foot close to the left foot. Eyes look to the right front (Figure 3-41).

3. 右腳向右前方邁出一步，腳跟著地。同時，兩前臂旋轉，左臂內旋，右臂外旋，兩掌翻轉，屈臂上舉，兩掌心相對，收於胸前。頭隨身體自然轉動（圖3-42）。

(3) The right foot takes a step to the right front, the heel touching the ground. Meanwhile, rotate the left arm inward and the right arm outward. Turn over both palms, and bend the arms in front of the chest, palms facing to each other. Turn the head naturally to follow the body (Figure 3-42).

4.右腳落實，身體重心前移成右弓步。兩臂同時向前擠出，兩臂撐圓，左掌指貼近右腕，掌心向外，指尖斜向上；右掌心向內，指尖向左，高與肩平。眼看右腕，成右捋擠式（圖3-43）。

(4) Land the right foot on the ground firmly. Shift the weight forward to form a right Bow Step. Push both hands forward at the same time, arms arched. Attach the left palm to the right wrist with the palm facing outward and the fingers pointing diagonally up. The right palm faces inward and the fingers, at shoulder level, point to the left. Eyes look at the right wrist. This is "Push and Pull" on the right (Figure 3-43).

5.身體重心向後移，右腳尖蹺起，微向內扣，再落地成右弓步。同時，上體左轉，左掌自右前臂上方

圖3-42　　　　　圖3-43　　　　　圖3-44

穿出，向左前方畫弧平抹；右掌微向後畫弧，收至左肘內側下方。眼看左掌（圖3-44、圖3-45）。

(5) Shift the weight backward. Tilt the toes of the right foot up and swing them slightly inward, and then land the right foot on the ground to form a right Bow Step. Meanwhile, turn the upper body to the left; thrust the left palm above the right forearm and draw an arc levelly to the left front. The right hand draws a small arc backward and stops under the left elbow. Eyes look to the left hand (Figure 3-44, Figure 3-45).

6. 左挒擠式動作同前右挒擠式，唯左右相反（圖3-46～圖3-48）。

(6) Repeat (2), (3), (4) in opposite directions (Figure 3-46～Figure 3-48).

圖3-45　　　　　圖3-46　　　　　圖3-47

7. 右捋擠式動作同前右捋擠式（圖 3-49～圖 3-53）。

(7) Repeat (2), (3), (4)in the same directions (Figure 3-49～Figure 3-53).

圖3-48　　　　　圖3-49　　　　　圖3-50

圖3-51　　　　　圖3-52　　　　　圖3-53

【要點】

由挒變擠時，兩掌在體前邊翻轉邊上提，兩手擺動不要超過身體。下挒與收腳，前擠與弓腿要做到協調一致。收腳時，如果初學者重心不穩，腳前掌可以在支撐腳內側點地停頓一下，然後再向前上步。類似動作皆同樣處理。

Key Points

As the "Push" is following the "Pull", turn both palms over before the body and rise up at the same time. Do not move the hands beyond the head. Coordinate pulling the hands and drawing in the feet with each other, as well as pushing the hands and bending the legs. When drawing in the feet, as a beginner, one may stand unsteadily; let the ball of the foot pause by the support-ing foot, and then step forward. This also applies to similar movements.

十、左搬攔捶

【訣要】

先搬後攔是搬攔，先攔後搬是攔搬；
這捶加在搬攔內，乘機擊打無後先；
四平擊去在中脘，上撞天突下載丹；
左右膺窗擊中凶，肋骨兩邊命不存。

10. Deflect, Parry and Punch – Left

Highlight

Deflect first, then parry, or vice versa.

A punch is hidden;

seize the right opportunity and strike quickly

Hit his stomach,

abdomen or Tian Tu Xue

(an acupuncture point between the chest and throat).

A hit to his left or right ribs is a possible,

but perhaps fatal strike.

1. 緊接上式，身體重心向後移動，右腳尖外展，上體向右撐轉。左掌向左前方伸展，掌心斜向下；右掌同時向下畫弧，掌心向上。眼看左掌（圖3-54）。

（1）Shift the weight backward. Turn the toes of the right foot outward and twist the upper body to the right. Extend the left hand to the left front, palm facing diagonally down. Draw the right hand in an arc downward at the same time, palm facing up. Eyes look at the left hand (Figure 3-54).

2. 身體重心前移，左腳收於右腳內側。右掌自下向後畫弧，再向上捲收，停於體前，掌心向下，高與肩平；左掌向下、向右畫弧收於右腹前，掌心向上。
眼向前平視（圖3-55）。

（2）Shift the weight forward. Move the left foot close to
the right foot. The right palm first draws an arc backward, then
upward, and stops in front of the body at shoulder level, palm
facing down. The left palm draws an arc downward and backward,
then stops before the abdomen to the right, palm facing up.
Eyes look forward（Figure 3-55）.

3. 左腳向前上步，腳跟著地，腳尖外撇。左掌隨
之向前搬出，掌心向上，高與胸平，右掌經左前臂外
側順勢按至右胯旁。眼看左掌（圖3-56）。

（3）The left foot steps forward with heel touching the
ground and toes turning outward. Throw the left palm forward,

圖3-54　　　　圖3-55　　　　圖3-56

palm facing up at chest level. Move the right palm along the outside of the left forearm and press it down at the side of the right hip. Eyes look at the left fist (Figure 3–56).

4. 身體重心前移，左腳落實，右腳於左腳內側收提上步，腰向左擰轉。左掌變拳向左畫弧收於左腰側，拳心向上；右掌經體右側畫弧向前攔出，高與胸齊，掌心向前下方。眼看右掌（圖3–57）。

(4) Shift the weight forward. Step the left foot on the ground solidly. Bring the right foot to the left foot and step forward. Turn the waist to the left. The left fist draws an arc to the left and stops at the left side of the waist, palm facing up. The right palm draws an arc forward along the right side of the body to parry in front of the chest, palm facing the lower front. Eyes look

圖3-57   圖3-58

to the right palm (Figure 3–57).

5. 身體重心向前移動成右弓步。左拳由腰間向前打出，拳眼向上，高與胸齊，右掌同時收於左前臂內側。眼看左拳（圖3–58）。

(5) Shift the weight forward to form a right Bow Step. Punch with the left fist forward, up to the chest level, the fist eye pointing up. Meanwhile, withdraw the right hand back to the left forearm. Eyes look to the left fist (Figure 3–58).

【要點】
兩手畫弧相交時前後上下要對稱，畫成兩個相交的立圓。左拳推出後再回收時，左前臂先內旋，然後再外旋，捲收於腰間；右掌攔出時，右前臂先外旋，然後再內旋並攔於體前。

Key Points

When drawing circles with two hands, keep them symmetrical, and cross them like a Venn diagram. While drawing back the left fist after striking, first rotate the left forearm inward, then outward, and draw it back to the waist. While deflecting with the right palm, first rotate the right forearm outward, then inward, and stop in front of the body.

十一、左攬雀尾

【訣要】

出手含似掤圍牆，雖遇強敵莫慌張；

變個圈兒左右畫，後腿挺勁作中樑；

掤将擠按須認真，上下相隨人難進；

任他勁力來打我，牽動四兩撥千斤；

引進落空合即出，沾黏連隨不丟頂；

攔雀尾勢推四正，屈伸開合妙無窮；

世人練得圈中妙，真能四兩撥千斤。

11. Grasping Bird's Tail – Left

Highlight

Push with the power of destroying a wall;

not fear even a stronger enemy,

Draw circles left and right at your will;

strong support comes from the back leg.

Pulling and pushing accordingly;

allow none to approach.

As the opponent strikes,

lead him in and redirect him out.

Push or pull according to the direction of the enemy's strike;

no one can escape.

Alternate bend and stretch or open and close,

which creates the real magic.

If one uses the magic well,

he can beat a more powerful enemy with very little effort.

1. 緊接上式，上體後坐，右腳尖外展，腰向右擰轉。右前臂外旋，右掌向下畫弧，掌心向上；左拳變掌，前臂內旋並前伸，掌心轉向下（圖3-59）。

（1）Move the upper body backward. Turn the toes of the right foot outward and the waist to the right. Rotates the right forearm outward, and draw the hand downward in an arc, palm facing up. Change the left fist into an open palm. Rotate the forearm inward and stretch it forward, palm facing down (Figure 3-59).

圖3-59

2.右腳落實，身體重心前移，左腳收於右腳內側。同時，左掌由前向下畫弧至腰間，右掌自下向後、向上畫弧收捲至胸前，兩掌成抱球狀（圖3-60）。

(2) Land the right foot on the ground solidly and shift the weight forward. Bring the left foot close to the right foot. Meanwhile, move the left hand to draw an arc downward to the waist. The right hand draws an arc upward and backward and rolls back in front of the chest. Two palms are corresponding as if holding a ball (Figure 3-60).

3.上體微左轉，左腳向前邁出一步，身體重心前移，右腿後蹬，腳跟後展，成左弓步。同時，左前臂向前出，高與肩平，掌心向內，右掌向下按於右胯旁。眼看左前臂（圖3-61）。

圖3-60   圖3-61   圖3-62

(3) Turn the upper body to the left. Move the left foot a step forward and shift the weight forward too. Extend the right leg backward and stretch the heel backward to form a left Bow Step. At the same time, push the left forearm upward to the shoulder level, palm facing inward. Press the right hand down by the right hip. Eyes look at the left forearm (Figure 3-61).

4. 腰微向左擰轉，左掌前伸並翻掌，掌心向下；右前臂外旋，掌心轉向上，經腹前向上、向前伸至左前臂下方（圖3-62）。

(4) Slightly twist the waist to the left. Move the left hand forward and turn it over, palm facing down. Rotate the right forearm outward, and turn the palm to face up. Move the right hand upward and forward in front of the abdomen and stop it under the left forearm (Figure 3-62).

5. 上體向右擰轉，兩掌向下将回並經腹前向右後上方畫弧，右掌心斜向上，左前臂平屈於胸前。同時，上體後坐，右腿屈膝，身體重心偏於右腿。眼看右掌（圖3-63）。

(5) Twist the upper body to the right. Pull back both hands and draw an arc past the abdomen to the upper right back, the right palm facing diagonally up and the left forearm bending levelly

before the chest. Meanwhile, move the upper body backward, bend the right knee, and shift the weight mainly onto the right leg. Eyes look at the right palm (Figure 3–63).

6.上體向左擰轉，面向正前方，身體重心前移成左弓步。右臂屈肘，右掌捲收，掌指向前搭近左腕，雙掌同時向前慢慢擠出，高與肩平，左掌心向內，右掌心向前，兩臂保持半圓形。眼看左腕（圖3-64）。

(6) Twist the waist to the left and face the front. Shift the weight forward to form a left Bow Step. Bend the right arm, roll back the hand, and bring the fingers onto the left wrist. Push both hands forward slowly, up to the shoulder level, the left palm facing inward and the right palm facing forward, arms arched. Eyes look at the left wrist (Figure 3–64).

圖3-63　　　　　　圖3-64

7. 右掌經左腕上方伸出，兩掌向左右分開，與肩同寬，掌心均向下。隨即上體後坐，身體重心移至右腿，左腳尖蹺起。兩臂屈肘，雙掌收至胸前，掌心均向前下方。眼平視前方（圖3-65）。

（7）Extend the right palm above the left wrist and separate the hands sideways until they are shoulders width apart, palms facing down. Then move the upper body backward. Shift the weight onto the right leg. Tilt the toes of the left foot up. Bend the elbows and draw the hands back to the front of the chest, both palms facing the lower front. Eyes look forward (Figure 3–65).

8. 左腿前弓成左弓步。兩掌下落經腹前向前、向上按出，腕高與肩平。鬆腰鬆胯，沉肩墜肘，塌腕舒掌。眼平視前方（圖3-66）。

圖3-65　　　　　　　圖3-66

(8) Bend the left leg to form a left Bow Step. Both palms fall down before the abdomen and then push forward and upward, wrists at shoulder level. Relax the waist and hips; sink the shoulders, elbows and wrists. Stretch the palms. Eyes look forward (Figure 3–66).

【要點】

由捋變擠時，兩手向身後擺開；由擠變按時，注意縮胯，斂臀，上體正直，不可前俯後仰。

Key Points

When changing from pulling to pushing, pull both hands backward behind the body. When changing from pushing to pulling, pay attention to pull the hips and the buttocks in; keep the upper body upright. Do not lean forward or backward.

十二、十字手

【訣要】

左手採來右手提，緊貼緊靠莫相離；
橫提要向當中去，變作雙峰貫耳宜。

12. Cross Hands

Highlight

The left hand plucks;

the right hand lifts；

the two are cooperating.

Strike on the enemy's middle

and prepare on his ears.

1. 接上式，身體重心移向右腿，左腳尖內扣，身體向右轉。右掌由左向右畫弧至身體右側，左掌對稱地分舉在身體左側，兩肘微屈，兩掌心均向前。眼看右掌（圖3-67）。

（1）Shift the weight onto the right leg. Turn the body to the right and swing the toes of the left foot inward. While the right hand draws an arc from left to the right and stop at the right side of the body, the left hand moves to the left side of the body symmetrically. Both arms bend slightly, palms facing

圖3-67　　　　　　圖3-68

forward. Eyes look at the right palm (Figure 3-67).

2. 身體重心移於左腿，右腳收於左腳內側。同時，右掌向下、向左畫弧至體前，高與肩平；左掌同時收至體前，與右掌腕部相交搭，抱成斜十字形，左掌在內，右掌在外，掌心都轉向內。眼看前方（圖3-68）。

(2) Shift the weight onto the left leg and bring the right foot close to the left foot. Meanwhile, the right hand draws an arc towards the back and left and stops in front of the body at the height of the shoulders. Draw back the left hand to the front of the body at the same time, overlapping with the right hand at the wrist to form an "X". The left hand is inside and the right hand is outside, both palms facing inward. Eyes look forward (Figure 3-68).

【要點】

上下肢動作要協調一致，一氣呵成。

Key Points

The movement is seamless. The upper limbs and lower limbs are coordinated with each other.

十三、斜身靠

【訣要】

其法分肩背，斜飛勢用肩，肩中還有背；

一旦機會乘，轟然如倒碓，不丟我中心；

百使百成功，姿勢若有偏，失中徒無功。

13. Lean the Body and Push with the Shoulder

Highlight

Push the enemy with the shoulder and the back.

Knock him down while keeping yourself balanced.

Otherwise, you will fail for sure.

1. 上體微向右擰轉，右腳向右前方邁出一步，腳跟著地。同時，兩手握拳，前臂向內旋。眼看前方（圖3-69）。

（1）Slightly twist the upper body to the right. The right foot takes a step to the right front, heel touching the ground.

圖3-69　　　　　　圖3-70

Meanwhile, form fists with both hands. Rotate both forearms inward. Eyes look ahead (Figure 3–69).

2. 身體重心向前移動，左腿自然蹬直，腳跟隨之後展，成右弓步。同時，兩拳分別向左下和右上撐開，右拳停於右額角前，拳心斜向外；左拳下撐於左胯旁，拳心斜向身後。眼看左前方（圖3–70）。

(2) Shift the weight forward. Extend the left leg naturally straight and stretch the heel backward to form a right Bow Step. At the same time, separate the fists, the left fist to the lower left and the right to the upper right. The right fist stops in front of the right forehead, palm facing diagonally outward. The left fist stops at the side of the left hip, palm facing diagonally backward. Eyes look to the left front (Figure 3–70).

【要點】
注意沉肩鬆胯，肩、臂向外撐勁，上體不要側倒。

Key Points

Sink the shoulders and elbows. Relax the hips. Push the arms and shoulders outward. Do not lean in any direction.

十四、肘底捶

【訣要】

捶居肘下勢堪誇，好似葉底下藏花；

專向敵人胸肋部，攔腰擊打兩不差；

敵勁來時順勁抓，執腕及扣落平沙；

倘然右手被人執，肘腕相搓破擒拿；

搓手蹲身勢有名，夾住敵臂任施行；

擒拿是我圈中妙，爾想逃脫不可能。

14. Fist under the Elbow

Highlight

A fist is hidden under an elbow,

like a flower under a leaf.

Punch the opponent's ribs, chest, or waist.

If he is striking,

grasp his wrist and punch him.

If your right hand is caught,

twist the elbow and the wrist to break free.

Move around the hand and lower the body;

clip his arm.

Catching is a trick;

no matter how hard he struggles,

escape is impossible.

1. 接上式，身體重心向左移動，右腳尖隨之蹺起並向內扣，上體左轉。右拳變掌，前臂外旋，掌心向上並向內掩裹畫弧；左拳同時變掌，向左、向內畫弧。眼看右掌（圖3-71）。

（1）Shift the weight to the left, and accordingly tilt the toes of the right foot up and turn them inward. Turn the upper body to the left. The right fist changes into an open palm. Rotate the right forearm outward, and move the palm upward and then inward. Meanwhile, the left fist changes into an open palm too and draws an arc to the left and inward. Eyes look at the right palm (Figure 3–71).

圖3-71　　　　圖3-72　　　　圖3-73

2. 身體重心向右移動，左腳收至右腳內側。右掌翻轉並屈收在右胸前，掌心向下；左前臂外旋，左掌掌心翻轉向上，並經腹前向右畫弧，與右掌相對成抱球狀，右掌在上，左掌在下。眼看右掌（圖3-72）。

（2）Shift the weight to the right. Move the left foot next to the right foot. Turn over the right hand and draw it back in front of the chest, to the right, palm facing down. Rotate the left forearm outward, turn over the left palm facing up, passing the abdomen to draw an arc rightward, corresponding with the right palm as if holding a ball; the right palm is above the left palm. Eyes look at the right palm (Figure 3–72).

3. 上體向左轉動，左腳向左前方擺腳墊步，腳跟著地，腳尖外擺。左掌經右前臂下方向左上方畫弧，掌心向內，高與鼻齊，右掌經左胸前畫弧下落至右胯旁。眼看左掌（圖3-73）。

（3）Turn the upper body to the left. The left foot skips to the left front, heel touching the ground, toes pointing outward. Move the left palm past the right forearm to draw an arc to the upper left, palm facing inward at nose level. The right palm draws an arc past the left chest down to the right hip. Eyes look at the left palm (Figure 3–73).

4. 上體繼續向左轉動，左腳落實，身體重心前移至左腿，右腳跟進半步，腳前掌著地，落在左腳後面。左前臂內旋，左掌向左、向下畫弧至體側，掌心向下；右掌向右、向前畫弧至體前，掌心斜向上，高與鼻平。面向正前方，眼看右掌（圖3-74）。

(4) Continue to turn the upper body to the left. Plant the left foot on the ground solidly and shift the weight forward onto the left leg. The right foot follows a half step, the ball of the foot touching the ground. The left forearm rotates inward and draws an arc leftward and downward to the side of the body, palm facing down. The right palm draws an arc to the right, then forward, and stops in front of the body, palm facing diagonally up at the height of the nose. With the face facing front, eyes look at the right palm (Figure 3-74).

圖3-74　　　　　　　　　　　圖3-75

5. 身體重心向後移動，右腳落實，左腳向前微移，腳跟著地成左虛步。左掌經腰際從右腕上向前穿出成側立掌，掌心向右，掌指向上，指尖與眉心相對；同時，右掌變拳收回，置於左肘內側下方。眼看左掌（圖3-75）。

（5）Shift the weight backward. Place the right foot on the ground solidly and move the left foot slightly forward with the heel touching the ground to form a left Empty Step. Thrust the left palm forward from the waist over the right wrist, palm facing right, fingers pointing up, and the fingertips are aligned with the glabellum （point between the eyebrows）. Meanwhile, the right palm changes into a fist and draws back to the lower inside of the left elbow. Eyes look at the left palm （Figure 3–75）.

【要點】

整個動作要連貫一致，一氣呵成，以腰為軸帶動四肢。定式時，鬆肩垂肘，微向下沉，右拳置於左肘下方偏右，保持胸部舒展。

Key Points

Using the waist to lead the limbs, the entire movement is seamless and smooth. When the movement is settled, relax the shoulders and sink the elbows. Place the right fist under the left elbow slightly to the right. Keep the chest stretched.

十五、倒攆猴

【訣要】

此勢因何號攆猴，輕身腳步快如流；

摟探帶引中盤下，指點掌印擊人頭；

身後有敵當中按，還須腰勁曲中求；

如逢步下鈎盤到，腳跟倒掛利如鈎；

步退掌進勢須平，蛇到常山別樣靈；

打到肋下擊腦後，才顯手段是高明。

15. Step Backward and Push

Highlight

Move backward gently and quickly.

Lead the enemy lower and closer;

then strike on his head by fingers or palm.

Use the force from the waist to strike on his middle

when he comes behind.

The heel is sharp like a hook.

Keep balance when step backward

and push hand forward, alert like a snake.

Strike his ribs and back of the head to show high skills.

1. 緊接上式，上體向右轉動，右拳變掌，掌心向上，經前經右胯側向後畫弧平舉，肘部微屈；隨之左臂外旋，掌心翻向上。左腳輕輕提起，眼隨轉體先向右看，再轉向前看左掌（圖3-76）。

（1）Turn the upper body to the right. The right fist turns into an open palm which faces up and passes the right waist to draw an arc backward, the elbow bending slightly. The left arm rotates outward and turns over to face up. Eyes follow the body to look to the right first, then the left hand (Figure 3-76).

2. 左腳輕提，腳尖下垂，向後退步，腳前掌著地，隨之身體重心後移，左腳踏實，右腳腳跟微向外展，腳尖朝前成右虛步。同時，右臂屈肘，右掌捲收經耳側向前推出，掌心向前，高與肩平，左手向下撤至左胯前。眼看右掌，上體正直，鬆腰鬆胯（圖3-77）。

圖3-76　　　　　　　圖3-77

(2) Lift the left foot lightly, toes pointing downward, and step backward, ball of the foot on the ground. Shift the weight backward and place the left foot on the ground. Swing the right heel outward, toes pointing forward to form a right Empty Step. Meanwhile, bend the right elbow, and push the right hand forward past the right ear, palm facing forward at shoulder level. Move the left hand down by the left hip. Eyes look at the right hand; keep the upper body straight; relax the waist and hips (Figure 3–77).

3. 上體左轉，左掌向下、向左後方畫弧平舉，掌心向上；同時，右臂外旋，掌心轉向上。眼隨轉體先向左看，再轉看右掌（圖3–78）。

(3) Turn the upper body to the left. The left hand draws an arc downward, then to the left back, palm facing upward. Meanwhile, rotate the right arm outward until the palm faces up. Eyes follow the body to look to the left first, then the right hand (Figure 3–78).

4. 右腳輕輕提起向後退步，腳前掌先落地，隨之全腳踏實，重心移至右腿；左腳腳跟微外展，左膝微屈成左虛步。左掌屈肘捲收經耳側向前推出，掌心向前，高與肩平，右掌向下、向後撤至右胯前。眼看左掌（圖3-79）。

（4）Lift the right foot lightly and step backward, placing the ball of the foot on the ground first, then the entire foot. Shift the weight onto the right leg. Swing the left heel outward, toes pointing forward to form a left Empty Step. Meanwhile, bend the left elbow, and push the left hand forward passing the left ear, palm facing forward at shoulder level. Move the right hand down by the right hip. Eyes look at the left hand（Figure 3-79）.

5. 倒攆猴左右各重複一次，動作同前（圖3-80～圖3-83）。

（5）Repeat（3）and（4）（Figure 3-80～ Figure 3-83）.

圖3-78　　　圖3-79　　　圖3-80

【要點】

退步時，腳前掌先著地，然後再全腳踏實，重心後移，做到虛實轉換清楚。同時，保持兩腳約10公分的橫向距離，不可兩腿交叉狀退步，以免重心不穩。

Key Points

When stepping backward, place the ball of the foot on the ground first, and then the entire foot. When shifting the weight backward, shift it from one leg to the other. Do not align or cross the feet. Keep the weight stable.

十六、斜四角推掌

【訣要】

撇身更帶一反身，專防敵人後面攻。

將手撲面尋常事，吐信傷面格外凶。

圖3-81　　　　圖3-82　　　　圖3-83

16. Push Diagonally

Highlight

Retreat and turn to protect yourself

from the enemy behind.

Pull back the hands and attack his face fiercely

like a snake striking with its tongue.

1. 接上式，左腳撤至右腳後，腳前掌著地。左掌外旋先向上舉，再收至右胸前，掌心向下；右掌由下向右上方畫弧，掌心向上，高與頭平。眼看右掌（圖3-84）。

（1）Place the left foot behind the right foot with the ball of the foot on the ground. Move the left hand outward and upward,

圖3-84

and then stop in front of the right chest, palm facing downward. The right hand draws an arc to the right front at head level, palm facing upward. Eyes look at the right hand (Figure 3-84).

2. 以左腳掌、右腳跟為軸向左後方轉體，轉身後身體重心仍在右腿。在轉動中右掌屈肘回收，左手略向下按右胯前。眼看左前方（圖3-85）。

（2）Use the left ball of the foot and right heel as axes and turn the body to the left back, the weight still on the right leg. Meanwhile, bend the right elbow and draw the hand back. Push the left hand slightly by the right hip. Eyes look to the left front (Figure 3-85).

3. 左腳前進邁步，右腳隨即跟進，落於左腳後面，腳前掌著地成丁字步。同時，左掌下落經左膝前摟過，按於左胯旁，掌指向前；右掌經耳側向前推出，掌指向上，掌心向前，指尖高與鼻平。眼看右掌（圖3-86）。

（3）The left foot takes a step forward and the right foot follows with the ball of the foot on the ground to form a T-Step. Meanwhile, the left hand falls to the knee and pulls back to the left hip, fingers pointing forward. The right hand pushes forward from the side of the ear, fingers pointing upward at nose level, palm facing forward. Eyes look at the right hand (Figure 3–86).

4. 右腳微後撤，踏實地面，身體重心落於右腿，左腳向內扣，上體向右後擰轉，轉身後身體重心移至左腿，右腳隨即輕提成丁虛步。同時，左臂外旋並向左、向上畫弧上舉，掌心向上，高與頭平；右掌下落至右胯前，掌心向下。眼看右前方（圖3–87）。

（4）Move the right foot backward slightly and place it on the ground solidly. Shift the weight onto the right leg. Swing the left foot inward. Turn the upper body to the right back, then shift the weight onto the left leg. Meanwhile, rotate the left arm outward, and draw an arc with it leftward and upward, palm facing upward at head level. The right hand falls down in front

圖3–85　　　　圖3–86　　　　圖3–87

of the right hip, palm facing downward. Eyes look to the right front（Figure 3–87）.

5. 右腳向前上步，左腳隨即跟進，落在右腳後面，腳前掌著地成丁字步。右掌經右膝前摟過，掌指向前，按於右胯旁；左掌經耳側向前推出，掌指向上，掌心向前，指尖高與鼻平。眼看左掌（圖3–88）。

（5）The right foot takes a step forward and the left foot follows the right with the ball of the foot on the ground to form a T–Step. Meanwhile, the right hand falls to the knee and pulls back to the right hip, fingers pointing forward. The left hand pushes forward from the outside of the ear, fingers pointing upward at nose level, palm facing forward. Eyes look at the left hand（Figure 3–88）.

6. 左右轉身推掌各重複一次，動作同前，唯方向相反，成四角形推掌（圖3–89～圖3–92）。

（6）Repeat（2），（3），（4），（5）in opposite direction（Figure 3–89 ～ Figure 3–92）.

【要點】
丁步時，兩腳橫豎均要保持約10公分的距離，以便於轉動。轉動時，體重置於兩腳間，轉身後重心移

向後腿，推掌時重心在前腿。整個動作要做到既輕靈
又穩重、沉實。

Key Points

When forming the T-Step, keep a distance of 10 cm between the feet in order to turn smoothly. When turning the body, keep the weight between the feet. After turning, shift the weight onto

圖3-88　　　　圖3-89　　　　圖3-90

圖3-91　　　　　　　圖3-92

the back leg. When pushing the hand, shift the weight onto the front leg. Make the entire movement light, quick and steady.

十七、右手揮琵琶

【訣要】

雙手緊抱一琵琶，拆幹剪腕用不差；

裏外圈兒由我畫，揮擊專會破擒拿；

上打玄關下打陰，中間便是虎搯心；

此種機關休洩露，一著傷人禍不輕。

17. Playing a Pipa(Chinese Lute) – Right

Highlight

Two hands are positioned as if holding a Pipa,

the purpose of which is to bend the enemy's body or wrist.

Draw circles with both hands to avoid being caught.

Strike on the enemy's head, crotch, or heart.

Do not use this movement rashly in case of injuring

a person and creating more conflict.

1. 緊接上式，左腳向後撤半步，身體重心移於左腿，上體向左擰轉。左臂屈收，左掌帶至左胸前，掌心斜向下；右掌隨之向前、向上畫弧至體前，掌心斜向左。頭隨體轉，眼平視（圖3-93）。

（1）The left foot takes a half step backward. Shift the weight onto the left leg. Twist the upper body to the left. Bend the left arm and draw the hand back in front of the left chest, palm facing downward diagonally. The right hand draws an arc forward, upward and stops in front of the body, palm facing the left diagonally. The head follows the body; eyes look straight forward (Figure 3–93).

2. 上體微右轉，右掌微向下沉，前臂微外旋，掌心向左成側立掌，指尖與眉心相對；左掌自左胸前向前合於右臂內側，掌心向右，與右肘相對。同時，右腳提起微移，腳跟著地，膝微屈，成右虛步。眼看右掌（圖3-94）。

（2）Turn the upper body to the right slightly. Sink the

圖3-93　　　　　　　　圖3-94

right hand and rotate the forearm outward slightly, palm facing left, fingers pointing up, and fingertips at eyebrow level. Move the left hand from the left of the chest, close to the right elbow, palm facing the right. Meanwhile, move the right foot slightly with the heel touching the ground, and bend the knee slightly to form a right Empty Step. Eyes look at the right hand (Figure 3–94).

【要點】

定式時，兩臂輕輕沉合，注意正頭，豎頸，鬆腰，沉肩，上體正直。

Key Points

When the movement is settled, sink the arms and intend to push them together without actually doing so. Keep the head, neck and upper body straight. Relax waist. Sink the shoulders.

十八、跟步捋擠

【訣要】

引近我身邊，順其來勢攻，導之使長延。
輕靈不丟頂，力盡自然空，重心需自持。
莫被他人乘，擠時有兩方，直接單純意。
迎合一動中，間接反應力，如球撞壁還。
又如錢投鼓，咚咚聲鏗然。

18. Step up, Pull and Push

Highlight

Let the enemy get close;

pull him in the same direction of his attach; lead him further.

Pull and ready to push at any time; keep yourself stable.

Do not give him a chance.

Push when he tries to escape;

use his own force to attack him like a ball rebounding

from a wall or a coin on the drum:

quickly and forcefully.

1. 接上式，上體向左擰轉，右腳收回左腳前，腳尖點地。兩掌下捋至腹前，兩掌心斜相對。頭隨體轉，眼向前平視（圖3-95）。

（1）Twist the upper body to the left. Place the right foot in front of the left foot, toes touching the ground. Move both hands down to the stomach, right palm facing downward and left palm facing upward. The head follows the body and eyes look straight ahead (Figure 3-95).

2. 右腳前進半步，身體重心向前移至右腿，隨之左腳跟進落於右腳後面，腳前掌著地。兩掌翻轉提到胸前，同時向右、向前畫平弧，右掌心向上，高與肩平，左掌心向下附於右腕內側。眼看右掌（圖3-96、圖3-97）。

（2）The right foot takes a half step forward. Shift the weight onto the right leg. Place the left foot right behind the right foot, the ball of the foot on the ground. Both hands turn over and rise to chest level. Push both hands to the right front at shoulder level, right palm facing inward and upward, left hand residing at the right wrist. Eyes look at the right hand（Figure 3-96, Figure 3-97）.

【要點】

上下肢運動要協調一致，要用腰勁帶動四肢。

圖3-95　　　　　圖3-96　　　　　圖3-97

Key Points

The upper limbs and lower limbs are coordinated with each other. Use the waist to lead the limbs.

十九、上步栽捶

【訣要】

栽捶原向鬢間打，左手搬扣且擒拿；
待他左手迎拳來，栽下丹田用不空；
有時左手被擒拿，順頸栽擊不怕他；
拳到丹田施抖勁，管叫強敵落平沙；
將擠以後進前捶，箭步飛身更擊催；
敵已倒時猶不放，捷如閃電快似雷；
將擠還能迎敵蹬，吃甚還甚是常情；
捉拳栽下三焦去，攻變守來守變攻。

19. Step up and Punch

Highlight

The right hand punches the enemy's temple;

the left hand is parrying and grasping.

If his left hand blocks you,

then punch his abdomen.

If he captures your left hand,

then punch his neck.

A quick strike to his abdomen would make him fall.

After pulling and pushing,

step up fast and punch.

Beat him harder, when he is falling.

If he is kicking, pull his leg and pay him back.

Alternate offense and defense.

1. 緊接上式，身體重心移向左腿，上體向左擰轉。左前臂外旋，左掌向下、向後畫弧上舉，掌心斜向上，高與頭平；右掌經面前向左畫弧，按於左胸前，掌心向下。眼看左掌（圖3-98）。

（1）Shift the weight onto the left leg. Twist the upper body to the left. Rotate the left forearm outward and move the hand downward and backward in an arc, palm facing upward diagonally at head level. The right hand draws an arc to the left pass the face, and presses down to the left side of the chest, palm facing downward. Eyes look at the left hand（Figure 3-98）.

2. 上體向右擰轉，右腳向前邁步，踏實，左腿蹬直成右弓步。右掌向下經右膝前摟過，按於右胯旁，掌心向下，掌指向前；左掌變拳經耳側向前下方打出，拳眼向右，拳面斜向前下，高與腹平。眼看前下方（圖3-99）。

（2）Twist the upper body to the right. The right foot takes a step forward, and the left leg extends to form a right Bow Step. Move the right hand around the right knee, and press it by the side of the right hip, palm facing downward, fingers pointing forward. Turn the left palm into fist. Push the left fist from the outside of the ear to the lower front, palm facing downward diagonally at abdomen level. Eyes look to the lower front（Figure 3-99）.

【要點】

動作銜接力求圓活，要以腰帶動。定式時，上體不可過於前傾，步型為拗弓步。凡拗弓步步型，要注意保持兩腳較大跨度，做到重心穩定，上體自然正直。

圖3-98　　　　　　　　圖3-99

48式養生太極拳

Key Points

Use the waist to lead the movement and move smoothly. Do not lean the upper body forward. The steps are twisted in Bow Steps. Keep even steps. Keep the body stable and the upper body straight upright.

二十、轉身白蛇吐信

【訣要】

白蛇吐信甚為強，轉身撲面敵難防。

摟手搬扣兼進步，額下猶餘一掌藏。

鎖喉直撲脖間擒，胸要合來背要沉。

反手推擲多得勢，變作伏虎人難進。

20. Snake Turns and Puts out his Tongue

Highlight

This movement is powerful.

Turn your body and strike the enemy's face;

be blocked by nothing.

Step up with one hand parrying

and the other hiding under the chin.

Sink the back and draw in the chest,

attack his neck or throat.

Turn the body and push,

like a tiger allowing none to approach.

1. 接上式，身體重心向後移動，右腳尖蹺起。左拳上提，右掌上托。眼看右掌（圖3–100）。

（1）Shift the weight backward. Lift the toes of the right foot. The left fist rises, and the right hand lifts with the palm facing upward. Eyes look at the right hand (Figure 3–100).

2. 右腳內扣，向左後方轉體，身體重心轉向右腿，左腳提起原地向外擺腳，右腳跟隨轉體離地扭轉，兩腿交叉相送，右膝蓋接近左腿膝窩成歇步。左拳變掌經體前下落，收至腰間，掌心向上，掌指向前；右掌經耳側向前推出，高與胸平，掌心向前，掌指斜向上。眼看右掌（圖3–101）。

圖3–100   圖3–101

（2）Swing the toes of the right foot inward. Turn the body to the left back. Shift the weight onto the right leg. Lift the toes of the left foot and swing them outward. The right foot follows the body and turn to the left. Push both legs together, the right knee touching the inside of the left knee to form a Lower Squat with Legs Crossing. The left fist turns into an open palm and falls to left side of the waist, palm facing up, fingers pointing forward. The right hand pushes forward from the outside of the ear, at chest level, palm facing forward, fingers pointing up diagonally. Eyes look at the right hand（Figure 3-101）.

3. 身體重心前移，右腳提起向前上步，腳尖外擺，上體向右擰轉，左腳跟隨轉體離地扭轉，兩腿交叉相迭成歇步。左掌向後、向上捲收並經耳側向前推出，掌心向前，掌指斜向上，高與胸平；右掌翻轉向下、向後收至腰間，掌心向上，掌指向前。眼看左掌（圖3-102、圖3-103）。

（3）Shift the weight forward. The right foot takes a step forward, toes outward. Twist the upper body to the right. The left foot follows the body. Push both legs together, the right knee touching the inside of the left knee to form a Lower Squat with Legs Crossing. Move the left hand backward and upward then push it forward from the outside of the ear, palm facing forward, fingers pointing up at chest level. Turn the right hand to face down and move it to the right side of the waist, palm facing up, fingers pointing forward. Eyes look at the left hand (Figure 3–102, Figure 3–103).

【要點】

左腳向外擺轉時，應原地提起，然後橫落體前。轉身和上步時，要保持上體正直，不要歪扭。歇步時，兩腿半蹲，後膝接近前膝窩處，身體重心略偏於前腿。

Key Points

When swinging the left foot, lift it first, and then place in front of the body, toes pointing outward. When turning the body or taking a step, keep the upper body straight; do not lean or

圖3-102　　　　　　圖3-103

bend. When making a Lower Squat with Legs Crossing, both legs are in a half squat. The back knee touches the inside of the front knee. The weight is mostly on the front leg.

二十一、左右拍腳伏虎

【訣要】

猛虎撲來勢更凶，將他引進落成空；

搬打相隨傷耳鬢，通天一炮血花紅；

敵來握臂是雙手，後撤上轉黏即走；

引得敵跟提起後，探拳如箭擊迎頭。

21. Pat the Foot and catch a Tiger – Left and Right

Highlight

If the enemy pounces on you like a tiger,

trick him into getting close and dodge fast.

He will fall on the ground.

Punch his temples.

If he catches your arm,

stick on him and give him a push.

After his heels are off the ground,

punch his forehead like an arrow.

1. 緊接上式，重心前移，左腳向前墊步。左掌向左下方畫弧，右掌向後、向上畫弧，停於頭右側準備拍腳。眼向前平視（圖3-104）。

（1）Shift the weight forward. The left foot skip forward. The left hand draws an arc downward. The right hand draws an arc backward and upward, and stops at the right side of the head ready to pat the foot. Eyes look straight forward (Figure 3-104).

2. 左腳落實，左腿支撐，右腳向前、向上踢起，腳面自然伸平。右掌向前擊拍右腳面，左掌向後、向上畫弧，平舉於身體左後方，掌心向外，高與肩平。眼看右掌（圖3-105）。

（2）Place the left foot on the ground, with the left leg supporting the weight. The right foot kicks forward and upward,

圖3-104　　　　　　圖3-105

the foot stretched naturally. The right hand pats on the right foot at the back. The left hand draws an arc backward and upward, and stops behind the body at shoulder level, palm facing outward. Eyes look at the right hand (Figure 3-105).

3. 右腳向左前方落下，左腳在右腳落地之際隨即提起。同時，兩掌一起向右平擺，掌心均向下。眼看右掌（圖3-106）。

(3) The right foot falls on the ground in left front of the body. At the same time, lift the left foot. Move both hands to the right, both palms facing downward. Eyes look at the right hand (Figure 3-106).

4. 左腳向左側落步，右腿蹬直成左弓步。兩掌隨

圖3-106　　　　　　　　　圖3-107

左轉體經腹前向下、向左畫弧，邊畫弧邊握拳。眼看左拳（圖3-107）。

(4) The left foot falls on the ground at the left side of the body. Stretch the right leg to form a left Bow Step. Both hands follow the body and draw arcs in front of the abdomen downward and leftward and form fists. Eyes look at the left hand (Figure 3-107).

5. 上式不停，左拳向右屈肘平貫，停於左額前，拳心斜向外；右拳向左平貫，停於左肋前，拳心斜向下。鬆腰，鬆胯，眼轉看右前方（圖3-108a、圖3-108b）。

(5) Bend the left elbow and move the fist to the right until it is at the left side of the forehead, palm facing outward diagonally.

圖3-108a　　　　圖3-108b

Move the right fist to the left and stop by the left ribs, palm facing downward diagonally. Relax waist and hips. Eyes look to the right front (Figure 3–108a, Figure 3–108b).

6. 身體重心向後移動，左腳尖內扣，上體向右擰轉。同時，兩拳變掌，左掌收於胸前，掌心斜向上；右掌掌心斜向下，從左前臂上方穿出。眼平視前方（圖3–109）。

(6) Shift the weight backward. Swing the toes of the left foot inward. Twist the upper body to the right. Meanwhile, both fists become open palms. Draw the left hand back in front of the chest, palm facing upward diagonally. The right palm faces downward diagonally and thrusts forward over the left forearm. Eyes look straight forward (Figure 3–109).

7. 身體向左移動，重心移於左腿，右腳提起經左腳內側向前墊步。左掌向下、向後、向上畫半個圓，至頭左側，掌心向前，準備拍腳；右掌向前、向下畫半個立圓，停於右胯旁。眼向前平視（圖3–110、圖3–111）。

(7) Shift the upper body and the weight to the left. The right foot skips forward. The left hand draws an half circle downward, backward and upward, until it is at the left side of

the head, palm facing forward, ready to pat the foot. The right hand draws an arc forward and downward, and stops at the right hip. Eyes look straight forward (Figure 3–110, Figure 3–111).

8. 右腿支撐身體重心，左腳向前、向上踢起，腳面自然伸平。左掌向前擊拍左腳面，右掌向後、向上畫弧，平舉於身體右後方，高與肩平，掌心向下。眼看左掌（圖3-112）。

（8）The right leg supports the weight. The left foot kicks forward and upward, the foot stretched naturally. The left hand pats the back of the left foot. The right hand draws an arc backward and upward, and stops behind the body at shoulder level, palm facing downward. Eyes look at the left hand (Figure 3–112).

圖3-109　　　圖3-110　　　圖3-111

9. 左腳向右前方蓋步落地，右腳在左腳落地之際隨即提起。同時，兩掌一起向左平擺，兩掌心向下。眼看左掌（圖3-113）。

(9) The left foot falls on the ground in right front of the body. At the same time, lift the right foot. Move both hands to the left, both palms facing downward. Eyes look at the left hand (Figure 3-113).

10. 右腳向右側落步，右腿屈膝成右弓步。兩掌經腹前向下、向右畫弧，逐漸變拳。眼看正前方（圖3-114）。

(10) The right foot falls on the ground at the right side of the body. Bend the right leg to form a right Bow Step. Both hands follow the body and draw arcs in front of the abdomen

圖3-112　　　　　圖3-113

downward, rightward and turn into fists. Eyes look forward (Figure 3–114).

11. 上式不停，右拳向左屈肘平貫，停於右額前，拳心斜向外；左拳向右平貫，停於右肋前，拳心斜向下。鬆腰，鬆胯，眼轉看左前方（圖3–115）。

（11）Bend the right arm and move the fist to the right until it is at the right side of the forehead, palm facing outward diagonally. Move the left fist to the right and stop it by the right ribs, palm facing downward diagonally. Relax the waist and hips. Eyes look to the left front（Figure 3–115）.

【要點】

拍腳前，兩臂動作要與上步動作協調配合，不可

圖3–114　　　　　　　　圖3–115

上下脫節，也不要挺胸直臂。拍腳時，支撐腿微屈站穩，拍腳高度因人而異，不可彎腰憋氣，強求高度；拍腳後，先折收小腿再蓋步落地。落地時要輕緩，不要有意騰空縱跳；落地點不宜太遠，應偏於側前方。拍腳後也可向身後插步落地，隨之向體側撤步轉體，接做伏虎勢。插步練法也要求落地輕緩，移步平穩。

Key Points

Before patting the foot, the arms are coordinated with the foot. Do not push the chest out. When patting the foot, bend the supporting leg slightly and stand stably. Do not bend the back or hold the breath. Do not stress yourself to kick higher. After the kick, bend the knee first, and then put it on the ground with a Gai Step (Toes are pointing outward) lightly and to the right or left slightly. Do not jump. Do not make a big step. Instead of putting the foot ahead of the body, you may put it behind the body, and then turn the body over. The rest of the movement is the same.

二十二、左撇身捶

【訣要】

撇身更帶一反身，專防敵人後面攻。

捋手撲面尋常事，吐信傷面格外凶。

22. Throw the Left Fist

Highlight

Get the right wrist ready.

Swing the left arm and draw

back the elbow to cover the ribs.

Retreat and turn to protect yourself

from the enemy behind.

Pull back the hands and attack his face fiercely

like a snake striking with its tongue.

1. 接上式，身體重心向後移動，右腳內扣，上體向左擰轉。同時，右拳變掌，掌心斜向上，收於胸前；左拳亦變掌，掌心斜向下，從右前臂上向前穿出。眼向前看（圖3-116）。

（1）Shift the weight backward. Swing the right foot inward. Twist the upper body to the left. Meanwhile, the right fist turns into an open palm in front of the chest, palm facing upward. The left fist turns an open palm and thrusts forward over the right arm, palm facing downward. Eyes look forward (Figure 3-116).

2. 右腳踏實，身體重心移於右腿。左掌微向上、向前畫弧，掌心向下；右掌向下、向後畫弧至右胯前，掌心向上。眼看左掌（圖3-117）。

（2）Place the right foot on the ground. Shift the weight onto the right leg. The left hand draws an arc upward and forward, and palm facing downward. The right hand draws an arc downward and backward and stops in front of right hip, palm facing upward. Eyes look at the left hand（Figure 3-117）.

3. 上體向右擰轉，左腳收至右腳內側。左掌下落變拳收於小腹前，拳心斜向內，拳眼向右；右掌向後、向上再向體前畫弧，翻掌向下，附於左前臂內側。眼看左前方（圖3-118）。

（3）Twist the upper body to the right. Place the left foot beside the right foot. The left palm falls and turns into a fist, stopping in front of the stomach, palm facing inward and down.

圖3-116　　　　圖3-117

The right palm draws an arc in front of the body, and turns to face downward, beside the inside of the left arm. Eyes look to the left front (Figure 3–118).

4. 上體微向左擰轉，左腳向左前方邁出，身體重心向前移動成左弓步。左拳上提經面前向前撇出，拳心斜向上，高與頭平，右掌須附於左前臂內側。眼看左拳（圖3-119）。

(4) Turn the upper body to the left slightly. The left foot steps forward. Shift the weight forward to form a left Bow Step. Throw the left fist forward in front of the body at head level, palm facing in and up. Place the right palm on the left forearm. Eyes look at the left hand (Figure 3–119).

圖3-118　　　　　　圖3-119

48式養生太極拳

【要點】

撇拳前，右腳內扣不要過大。左掌向正前方穿出。回收時，兩手交叉畫圓，左掌邊收邊握拳，不要做成将的動作。整體動作中要注意腰的轉動，做到周身協調完整。

Key Points

When throwing the fist, swing the right foot inward slightly. Withdraw both hands in arcs and turn the left hand into a fist at the same time. Do not be confused with the Pull movement. Use the waist to lead the whole body.

二十三、穿拳下勢

【訣要】

下勢原似地頭蛇，形如一蝶下尋花；

雙将半咧開半岔，後路窘時用不差。

23. Thrust the Fist and lower Body

Highlight

Crouch down like a snake,

or like a butterfly seeking a flower.

Lower the body, pull and tear;

this can also be used for an escape.

1. 身體重心後移，左腳尖蹺起微向外擺，上體稍向左轉。左拳變掌向上、向左畫弧，右掌向下、向右畫弧，兩掌心均向下。眼看左掌（圖3-120）。

（1）Shift the weight backward. Tilt the toes of the left foot up and swing them slightly outward. Turn the upper body to the left. Change the left fist into an open palm and draw an arc upward and leftward. Move the right palm in an arc downward and rightward. Both palms face down. Eyes look at left hand (Figure 3-120).

2. 上式不停，左腳落實，身體重心前移，右腳收於左腳內側。兩掌繼續畫立圓，同時逐漸握拳，左拳心向內收於腹前，右拳心向內合於面前。眼向前看（圖3-121）。

（2）Place the left foot on the ground solidly and shift the

圖3-120　　　　　　　圖3-121

weight forward. Bring the right foot close to the left foot. The two palms continue to draw vertical circles, and at the same time, change them into fists gradually. Move the left fist back to the abdomen, palm facing inward. The right fist stops in front of the face with the palm facing inward. Eyes look forward (Figure 3–121).

3. 右臂掩肘下落，左拳從右前臂外側上穿。同時，左腿屈蹲，右腿向右側伸出成右仆步。眼看右前方（圖3-122）。

(3) The right arm falls down, led by the elbow. The left fist moves upward along the outside of right arm. Meanwhile, bend the left leg, and extend the right leg to the right to form a right Crouch Step. Eyes look to the right front (Figure 3–122).

4. 上體右轉，右拳經腹前沿右腿內向右前方穿出，左拳向左後上方伸展，兩拳拳眼均轉向上。眼看右拳（圖3-123）。

(4) Turn the upper body to the right. The right fist thrusts along the right leg from the abdomen to the right front. The left fist extends upward from the back. The eyes of the fists face up. Eyes look at the right fist (Figure 3–123).

【要點】

左腳尖外展不要過大，右腳提收後可稍點地停頓。仆步時，要先屈蹲左腿，隨之右腿向右側仆出，然後轉體穿拳。兩腳要全腳踏實，腳跟不要掀起。老年人可以放高姿勢，左腿半蹲做成半仆步。

Key Points

Do not turn the toes of the left foot outward too much. After lifting and drawing in the right foot, place it slightly on the ground and pause for a short while. When forming the Crouch Step, first bend the left leg, crouch the right leg to the right, and then turn the body and thrust the fist. Both feet are solid on the ground. Avoid lifting the heels. The elderly can form the position a little higher and half squat the left leg to form a half Crouch Step.

圖3-122　　　　圖3-123

二十四、左右獨立撐掌

【訣要】

如是蛰龍升上天，鳳凰展翅立平原；

擎掌上托額仰面，提膝直撞下丹田；

步下連隨分進步，手中擒拿換陰陽；

金雞獨立問堪式，變化擎提最忌偏；

下額惟虛擎掌托，哪堪左右更提膝；

追魂索命休輕用，怕他高眠臥不起。

24. Lift the Hand and Stand on One Leg – Left and Right

Highlight

Like a dragon flying up to the sky

or a phoenix spreading its wings,

raise the palm over the head;

lift the knee to hit the opponent's lower abdomen.

Steps alternate from forward to backward

while hands change between Yin and Yang.

Stand straight on one leg; do not lean in any direction.

If the opponent is struck on his chin

with the hand and his abdomen

with the knee at the same time, he may never rise.

1. 身體重心前移，右腳尖外展，左腳尖內扣，左腳微伸直。同時，右拳略上挑，左拳稍向下落，兩拳拳眼仍保持向上。眼看前方（圖3-124）。

（1）Shift the weight forward. Turn the toes of the right foot outward and the toes of the left foot inward, the left foot slightly stretched. Meanwhile, move the right fist slightly up and the left fist slightly down, eyes of both fists pointing up. Eyes look forward（Figure 3-124）.

2. 右腳蹬地，左腳提起。右拳變掌微內旋，左拳變掌下落，經腰側向前、向上方穿出，掌心向下。眼看前方（圖3-125）。

（2）Push the ground with the right foot and lift the left foot. Change the right fist into an open palm, turning it inward slightly.

圖3-124　　　　　　圖3-125

Turn the left fist into an open palm, and move it downward, and then forward and upward from the waist. Both palms face down. Eyes look forward (Figure 3–125).

3. 身體起立，右腿微屈站穩，左腿屈膝提至體前，腳面展平，成右獨立式。同時，右掌按於右胯前，指尖向左；左掌從右前臂內側上穿並翻掌心向上，撐於頭前上方，指尖向右，掌心斜向上。眼看前方（圖3-126）。

（3）Stand on the right leg and bend it slightly. Lift the left leg up in front of the body to form a One Leg Stand Step (right), toes pointing down. At the same time, push the right palm down by the right hip, fingers pointing left. Thrust the left palm upward from the inner side of the right forearm until

圖3-126　　　　　　　圖3-127

it is over the head, palm facing diagonally up, and fingers pointing to the right. Eyes look forward (Figure 3–126).

4. 左腳向前落步，身體重心前移，左腳蹬地，右腳提至體前，腳面展平，成左獨立式。右前臂外旋，右掌掌心向內經體前從左前臂內側上穿，翻掌於頭頂上方，指尖向左，掌心斜向上；左掌下落按於左胯前，指尖向右。眼向前看（圖3–127～圖3–129）。

(4) Place the left foot on the ground in front of the body and shift the weight forward. Push off the ground with the left foot and lift the right foot up in front of the body, toes pointing down to form a One Leg Stand Step (left). Turn the right forearm outward, palm facing inward and thrust the right hand upward from the inner side of the left forearm until it is over the

圖3–128　　　　　　圖3–129

head, palm facing diagonally up, fingers pointing to the left. The left hand pushes down by the left hip, fingertips pointing to the right. Eyes look forward (Figure 3-127～Figure 3-129).

【要點】

獨立步時，支撐腿微屈，膝部不要僵挺。向上穿掌時，要配合腰部的輕輕旋轉。撐掌時，上體保持正直，頭向上頂，全身要放鬆。

Key Points

In the One Leg Stand Step, bend the supporting leg slightly and avoid a rigid knee. When raising the palms up, turn the waist slightly in accordance. When pushing palms upward, keep the body upright, hold the head up, and relax the whole body.

二十五、退步攬雀尾

【訣要】

出手含掤似圍牆，雖遇強敵莫慌張；
變個圈兒左右畫，後腿挺勁作中樑；
若逢剛勁倚逞強，順勁下捋敵難防；
左搬右攔傷人面，或按或捋自思量；
卦象乾住首萬物，禁止上手太剛強；
向下常將按勁先，敵雖剛強莫相干；

變挒變擠從君意，拔背含胸最忌偏；

掤按雙推須熟練，挒來擠去像坎離；

全憑腰腿作機關，剛柔相濟勢不偏；

上掤下挒隨肘變，陰陽配備最稱神；

屈伸開合妙難言，攔雀尾勢推四正；

世人練得圈中妙，真能四兩撥千斤。

25. Step Back to Pull the Bird's Tail

Highlight

Push with the power of destroying a wall;

not fear even a stronger enemy,

Draw circles left and right at your will;

strong support comes from the back leg.

Pulling and pushing are coordinated

from the top to the bottom;

allow none to approach.

As the opponent strikes,

lead him in and redirect him out.

Push or pull according to the direction

of the enemy's strike;

stick to him, no one can escape.

Do not move rashly;

do not lean in any direction.

Keep the body straight;

power comes from the strong waist and legs.

The movements seem soft but are forceful.

Alternate bend and stretch or open and close,

which creates the real magic.

If one uses the magic well,

he can defeat a more powerful enemy with very little effort.

1. 右腳後撤一步，左腿屈蹲成左弓步。同時，右掌向前、向下落，掌心轉向上；左掌自右前臂上方向上、向前伸，掌心向下。眼看左掌（圖3-130）。

（1）Move the right foot a step backward, and bend the left leg to form a left Bow Step. Meanwhile, move the right hand forward and downward, palm facing up. Extend the left hand upward and forward over the right forearm, palm facing down. Eyes look at the left hand (Figure 3-130).

2. 身體重心向後移動，兩掌自體前向下、向後一起捋回，收至腹前，頭隨體轉（圖3-131）。

（2）Shift the weight backward. The two hands pull downward and backward and stop in front of the abdomen. The head follows the body (Figure 3-131).

3. 左掌經腹前翻轉上舉，高與胸平，掌心向內；右掌亦同時翻轉上舉，掌心向前，掌指附於左腕內側（圖3–132）。

(3) The left palm turns over and lifts up to the chest level, palm facing inward. At the same time, turn over the right palm and lift it up, palm facing forward, fingers at the inner side of the left wrist (Figure 3–132).

4. 身體重心向前移動，左腿屈膝前弓，上體向左擰轉。左掌自右向前畫平圓，高與肩平，掌心斜向內；右掌掌指附於左腕內側隨之畫圓。眼看左掌（圖3–133）。

(4) Shift the weight forward, bend the left knee, and turn the upper body to the left. The left palm, at the shoulder level,

圖3-130　　　圖3-131　　　圖3-132

draws a flat circle from the right to the front, palm facing diag-onally inward; the fingers of the right hand rest on the inner side of the left wrist and follow the left hand to draw a circle. Eyes look at the left palm (Figure 3–133).

5. 身體重心向後移動，左腳尖蹺起。左掌繼續屈肘向左、向後畫平圈，掌心翻向上，右掌隨之轉動。眼看左掌（圖3-134）。

（5）Shift the weight backward. Lift the toes of the left foot up. With the elbow bent, the left hand continues to draw a flat circle towards the left and back, palm turning over and facing up. The right hand follows. Eyes look at the left hand (Figure 3–134).

圖3-133　　　　　　　圖3-134

【要點】

弓步與推掌要協調，配合一致，胸部要舒展內含，肘、肩要鬆沉，手臂不要僵直，兩臂不要伸成一條直線。推掌時要走弧形，邊翻邊推，並與轉腰相配合。

Key Points

The Bow Step coordinates with the pushing hand. The chest is stretched and drawn in slightly. Relax the shoulders and elbows. Avoid stiff arms. Push hands in arcs and turn the palms over at the same time, which cooperate with the turning of the waist.

二十六、單鞭勢

【訣要】

單鞭一勢最稱雄，左像箭來右似弓；

鬆肩沉肘擋四面，鋼鞭一擊追人魂；

近得身來便是捌，或推或按任君施；

左顧右盼迎頭打，先擊敵人兩枝花。

26. Single Whip

Highlight

This posture makes you a true hero,

an arrow from the left, and a bow on the right.

Relax the shoulders and elbows to defend

and attack in all directions.

Strike powerfully as if holding a steel whip and scare the soul.

Pull when he comes close; be blocked by no one.

Beat directly; strike two birds with one stone.

1. 左腳尖內扣，身體重心移至左腿。左掌隨左前臂內旋向左前方按出，隨即變成勾手；右前臂微向外旋，右掌掌心轉向內，收於左肘彎處。同時，右腳收至左腳內側。眼看左勾手（圖3-135）。

（1）Turn the toes of the left foot inward. Shift the weight onto the left leg. With the forearm rotating inward, the left hand pushes towards the left front and forms a hook (Put all fingers and thumb together). Rotate the right forearm outward slightly. Turn the palm to face inward and draw it back by the left elbow. At the same time, place the right foot close to the left foot. Eyes look at the left hook (Figure 3–135).

2. 上體稍向右擰轉，右腳向右前方邁出一步，身體重心前移成右弓步。右掌隨著轉體慢慢翻掌並向前推出，掌指向上，掌心向前，指高與鼻平。右肘下垂於右膝，上下相對。眼看右掌（圖3-136）。

（2）Twist the upper body to the right slightly. Move the

right foot a step to the right front, and shift the weight forward to form a right Bow Step. Following the body, turn over the right palm slowly and push it forward, fingers pointing up, palm facing forward at nose level. The elbow is aligned with the right knee. Eyes look at the right hand (Figure 3–136).

【要點】

翻掌、推掌要協調一致，胸部要舒展內含，肘、肩要鬆沉，手臂不要僵直，兩臂不要伸成一條直線。推掌時，要走弧線，邊翻掌邊推，並與轉體動作相配合。到終點時，要沉肩塌腕，向下沉勁。

Key points

The palm turning over and the pushing hand should be co-ordinated with each other. Stretch the chest and draw it in

圖3-135　　　　　　　　圖3-136

slightly. Relax the shoulders and elbows. Avoid stiff and straight arms. Push hands in arcs and turn the palms over at the same time, cooperating with the turning of the waist. When the movement ends, sink the shoulders and wrist.

二十七、右雲手

【訣要】

> 提掛掤擲滾按推，全憑脊骨圓轉隨；
> 雲到敵人雙肋後，銅牆鐵柱一起推。

27. Cloud Hands – Right

Highlight

Lifting, blocking, pushing,

throwing and rolling all depend

on a strong spine and back.

When the hands move to the enemy's ribs,

push him forcefully.

1. 上體向左擰轉，身體重心移至左腿，右腳尖內扣。右掌向下、向左畫立圓至左肩前，掌心向內。眼看左勾手（圖3–137）。

（1）Twist the upper body to the left. Shift the weight onto the left leg and turn the toes of the right foot inward. Move the right hand to draw a vertical circle downward and leftward, and stop it in front of the left shoulder, palm facing inward. Eyes look at the left hook (Figure 3–137).

2. 右掌經面前向右繼續畫立圓，掌心向內；左勾手變掌，向下經腹前畫立圓。同時，左前臂外旋，掌心由外逐漸轉向內，身體重心漸漸移向右腿。上體和視線均隨右掌協調轉動（圖3-138、圖3-139）。

（2）The right hand continues to draw a vertical circle rightward in front of the face, palm facing inward. Turn the left hand into an open palm and move it in a circle downward in front of the abdomen. Meanwhile, rotate the left forearm outward to turn the palm gradually inward and shift the weight gradually onto the right leg. Both the upper body and eyes follow the right

圖3-137　　　　　圖3-138　　　　　圖3-139

hand（Figure 3–138, Figure 3–139）.

3. 上體繼續向右擰轉，右掌畫到身體右側，前臂內旋，掌心轉向面部；左掌向上畫弧至右肩前，掌心向內。同時，左腳向右腳靠攏，成開立步，兩腳相距一拳至兩拳之寬度，腳尖均向前。眼看右掌（圖3-140）。

（3）Continue to twist the upper body to the right. While the right hand moves to the right side of the body, the forearm rotates inward, palm facing inward. The left hand draws an arc upward to the right shoulder, palm facing inward. At the same time, move the left foot close to the right foot to form a Standing Apart Step （stand with the feet parallel）. The feet are a fist or two apart, toes pointing forward. Eyes look at the right hand （Figure 3–140）.

4. 上體向左擰轉，身體重心移向左腿。左掌經面前向左，右掌經腹前向左，同時畫立圓。上體和視線均隨左手轉動（圖3-141）。

（4）Turn the upper body to the left. Shift the weight onto the left leg. At the same time, both hands draw circles to the left, the left hand past the face and the right hand past the abdomen. The upper body and eyes follow the left hand （Figure 3–141）.

5. 上體繼續左轉，右腳向右側跨一步，腳尖仍向前。兩掌雲至身體左側時逐漸翻掌，左掌心轉向上，右掌心翻轉向下。眼看左掌（圖3-142）。

(5) Continue to turn the upper body to the left. The right foot takes a step to the right and the toes remain pointing forward. When the hands move to the left side of the body, both overturn gradually in order for the left palm to face upward and the right palm to face downward. Eyes look at the left hand (Figure 3-142).

6. 上體向右轉，身體重心移至右腳，左腳向右腳靠近，相距一拳至兩拳。右掌經面前向右，左掌經腹前向右，同時作立圓雲轉，雲至身體右側時，兩掌逐漸翻轉。上體和視線隨右手轉動（圖3-143、圖3-144）。

(6)Turn the upper body to the right. Shift the weight onto the

圖3-140　　　　圖3-141　　　　圖3-142

right leg. Move the left foot close to the right foot with a distance of one or two fists. Both hands draw circles to the right, the right hand past the face and the left hand past the abdomen. When the hands move to the right side of the body, both overturn gradually. The upper body and eyes follow the right hand (Figure 3–143, Figure 3–144).

7. 右雲手再重複一次，動作同前（圖3–145～圖3–148）。

（7）Repeat the above movements (Figure 3–145～Figure 3–148).

【要點】

兩腳要平行向右移動，開步和併步要輕提輕落，

圖3–143　　　圖3–144　　　圖3–145

腳前掌內側先著地。整個動作要均勻、平穩、協調、連貫，以腰為軸，上體要保持正直。兩掌雲轉時，上掌指高不過眉，下掌指低不過襠，翻掌不可突變，要邊畫圓邊翻轉。

Key Points

The feet stand parallel. Move the feet lightly with the balls of the feet on the ground first. Use the waist as an axle. The whole movement should be even, steady, seamless and coordinated. Keep the upper body upright. Do not move the hands higher than the eyebrow or lower than the crotch. Gradually turnover the hands while drawing circles.

圖3-146　　　圖3-147　　　圖3-148

二十八、野馬分鬃

【訣要】

雲手之後此勢連，左轉身來右手前；

縮身作了抱球式，樁步穿手如度遷；

或分或合闖東西，左右分披若千人；

不號斜飛憑腕力，專將捧力臂間通；

肩打肘靠腰如轉，拆幹剪腕肘撐身；

即引即擊待機勢，牽動四兩撥千斤。

28. Splitting Wild Horse's Mane

Highlight

After Cloud Hands comes this movement.

Turn the body to the left and lift the right hand.

Withdraw the body to position the hands as if holding a ball;

stand stable and thrust the hand forcefully.

Hands separate or reunite to strike in all directions

with the power of beating thousand enemies.

The power is from the wrist and up to the arm.

Strike his body or wrist with the shoulder or the elbow.

Seize a good opportunity;

beat a powerful enemy with a small effort.

1. 身體重心移至左腿，上體向左撐轉。兩掌繼續向左雲轉，至體前時，兩掌翻轉相對成抱球狀。同時，右腳輕輕提起。眼看左掌（圖3-149）。

（1）Shift the weight onto the left leg, and turn the upper body to the left. Move both arms to the left and turn them over when they are in front of the chest, palms facing each other as if holding a ball. Meanwhile, lift the right foot gently. Eyes look at the left hand (Figure 3-149).

2. 上體微向右轉動，右腳向右前方邁出一步，成右弓步，保持兩腳橫向距離約30公分。兩掌隨轉體分別向右上和左下分開，右掌指高與眼平，掌心斜向上；左掌按於左胯旁，掌心向下，指尖向前。眼看右掌（圖3-150）。

圖3-149　　　　　　　　3-150

（2）Slightly turn the upper body to the right. The right foot takes a step to the right front to form a right Bow Step. Following the turn of the body, separate the hands, the right palm facing diagonally up at eye level, the left hand by the left hip, palm facing down, fingers pointing forward. Eyes look at the right hand（Figure 3–150）.

3. 上體後坐，右腳尖外擺，上體微向右擰轉。右臂內旋，使掌心向下，左臂外旋，使掌心向上，兩掌右上左下在胸前成抱球狀。同時，左腳收於右腳內側，腳尖著地。眼看右掌（圖3–151、圖3–152）。

（3）Move the upper body backward and twist it to the right slightly. Turn the toes of the right foot outward. Rotate the right arm inward, palm facing down. Rotate the left arm outward, palm facing up. The right hand is at the upper right and the left hand is at the lower left in front of the chest, as if holding a ball. Meanwhile, move the left foot close to the right foot, toes touching the ground. Eyes look at the right hand（Figure3–151, Figure 3–152）.

4. 上體向左擰轉，左腳向左前方邁出一步，成左弓步，並保持兩腳橫向距離約30公分。兩掌隨轉體動作分別向左上和右下分開，左掌指高與眼平，掌心斜向上；右掌按於右胯旁，掌心向下，掌指向前。眼看左掌（圖3-153）。

（4）Twist the upper body to the left. The left foot takes a step to the left front to form a left Bow Step. Following the turn of the body, separate the hands, the left hand to the upper left and the right hand to the lower right, the left palm facing diagonally up at eye level, the right palm by the right hip, palm facing down, fingers pointing forward. Eyes look at the left hand (Figure 3-153).

【要點】

左右分鬃動作較前動作要開展一些，前腳稍向外斜，腰的扭轉幅度也較大些，所以，兩腳跨度應加大一些。弓步時，分掌和弓腿要協調一致，後腿邊蹬直，腳跟邊外展，兩腳夾角在45°～60°之間。類似動

圖3-151　　圖3-152　　　圖3-153

作都應如此處理。

Key Points

Compared to the movement in Pulling and Pushing, turn the front foot and the waist outward more and take a bigger step in the Bow Step. The separating hands and the bending legs are coordinated with each other. While straightening the back leg, the heel turns outward and forms an angle of 45° to 60° with the other foot. This rule applies to other similar movements.

二十九、高探馬

【訣要】

> 將手撲面濟陰陽，太極拳中此式良；
> 左右連環看手勢，步分順拗逞英豪；
> 搭手高攀在馬上，平肩正胯勢還藏；
> 進退變著要自然，輕靈神妙勢無雙。

29. Patting a High Horse

Highlight

Combining Yin and Yang,

this movement is the best in Tai Chi.

The hands correspond;

the steps move back and forth, alert.

Position the hands as if patting a horse.

The shoulders are flat,

the hips upright with peerless hidden power.

1.右腳跟進半步，腳掌著地。左掌微外展，右掌自下向後平舉，高與肩平，掌心向上。眼平視前方（圖3-154）。

（1）The right foot takes a half step forward, the ball of the foot on the ground. Extend the left hand slightly outward. Raise the right hand upward and backward, palm facing up at shoulder level. Eyes look forward (Figure 3-154).

2.身體重心向後移動，右腳隨之踏實，上體稍向右再向左撐轉，左腳稍向前墊步，腳前掌著地，成左虛步。左掌下落收至腰前方，掌心向上，掌指向前；

圖3-154　　　　　　　　圖3-155

右掌捲收經右耳旁向前推出，掌心斜向前，掌指高與眼平。眼看右掌（圖3-155）。

(2) Shift the weight backward. Plant the right foot on the ground. Twist the upper body slightly to the right and then to the left. Skip the left foot slightly forward, the ball of the foot touching the ground to form a left Empty Step. The left hand falls down in front of the waist, palm facing up, fingers pointing forward. Draw the right hand back and push it forward from the right ear, palm facing diagonally forward at the eyes level. Eyes look at the right hand (Figure 3–155).

【要點】

跟步、坐腿和墊步時，腳部要自然地微微左右轉動，防止前俯、撅臀和或高或低起伏。

Key Points

When taking the half step forward, or skipping or lowering the body, turn the feet to the left or right slightly and naturally. Do not lean forward, push hips out or move the body up or down.

三十、右蹬腳

【訣要】

搂打著力擊上盤，引他頭上若遮攔；

忽然蹬向胸面去，致命方知太極拳；

腿稱五行步五行，緩將進退顯屈伸；

只因及遠兼敵眾，踢在兩肋蹬在胸。

30. Kicking with the Right Heel

Highlight

Protect your own knees and strike his upper body.

When he uses his hands to parry,

kick his chest.

Step forward or backward slowly

and kick his ribs and chest.

This movement is used to fight a farer or more enemies.

1. 上體右轉，左腳輕輕提起。右掌向右後帶，左掌向左、向前畫弧（圖3–156）。

（1）Turn the upper body to the right. Lift the left foot up slightly. Draw the right hand to the right back. The left palm draws an arc leftward and forward（Figure 3–156）.

2. 左腳向左前方上半步，腳跟著地。同時，左前臂外旋，掌心向上，稍向後收，右掌自左前臂上方穿出。眼看右掌（圖3–157）。

（2）The left foot takes a half step to the left front, heel touching the ground. Meanwhile, the left forearm rotates outward with the palm facing up and draws backward slightly. The right palm thrusts over the left forearm. Eyes look at the right hand (Figure 3–157).

3. 左腳落實，身體重心向前移動，左腿前弓。右掌向上、向前畫圓，左掌向下、向後畫圓，右掌心、左掌心均向上。眼看右掌（圖3-158）。

（3）Place the left foot on the ground. Shift the weight forward. Bend the left leg to for a Bow Step. The right hand draws a circle upward and forward. The left hand draws a circle downward and backward. Both palms face up. Eyes look at the right hand (Figure 3–158).

4. 右腳收於左腳內側，腳尖點地，腰部稍向左再

圖3-156　　　　　　　　圖3-157

向右旋轉。右掌向下，左掌向上，同時繼續畫圓，至胸前時兩腕相交，兩掌合抱成斜十字，舉於胸前。右掌在外，左掌在內，兩掌心均向內。眼看右前方（圖3-159）。

（4）Bring the right foot back next to the left foot, toes touching the ground. Slightly turn the waist to the left, then to the right. Draw circles downward with the right hand and upward with the left hand. The two hands meet in front of the chest and form an "X", with the right hand on the outside and the left hand inside and both palm facing inward. Eyes look to the right front (Figure 3–159).

5. 左腿前屈，身體重心移至左腿，右膝隨即提起，右腳向右前方緩緩蹬出，腳尖蹺起，力在腳跟。

圖3-158　　　　　　圖3-159

兩掌分別向右前方和左後方畫弧撐開，肘部微屈，腕部高與肩平，兩掌心均向外，右臂、右腿上下相對。眼看右掌（圖3-160）。

(5) Bend the left leg and shift the weight onto it. Meanwhile, lift the right knee and kick the right foot slowly to the right front, delivering the force to the heel. The two hands draw arcs to the right front and the left back respectively, elbows bent, wrist at shoulder level, and palms facing outward. The right arm and right leg are aligned vertically. Eyes look at the right hand (Figure 3-160).

【要點】

蹬腿前，兩掌的轉換要與腰部旋轉相配合。掌的運行路線立圓和平圓要相互銜接，動作要圓活。兩掌

圖3-160

與蹬腳同時向斜前、斜後弧形撐開，不可直推猛撐。
蹬腳時，要勻要穩，上體保持自然正直，不要彎腰低
頭，勉強憋氣。

Key Points

Before kicking, move the hands coordinately with the waist.
The circles drawn by hands are connected smoothly. Along with
the hands, the kicking leg is stretched in arcs at the same
time. Avoid being rigid. When kicking, keep the upper body
naturally upright and stable. Do not bend waist, bow the head
or hold the breath.

三十一、雙峰貫耳

【訣要】

> 當胸敵來不需忙，順勢摟開貫耳掌；
> 身法一卸即不進，太陽擊中命歸陰；
> 雙峰貫耳莫猶疑，堂堂之陳正一旗；
> 上掤下摟隨時變，如電似雷真相宜；
> 敵若雙臂按前來，向上進步掤開捋；
> 順握雙臂欲何為，撤擊雙圈自解圍；
> 綿裏藏針憑迅速，最快無逾貫耳捶。

31. Striking Ears with Both Fists

Highlight

If a strike comes towards your chest,

block it then hit his ears with the fists.

Be as rapid as a lightning,

nothing can compare.

If the enemy pushes you with both arms,

step up, grasp his arms and ward him off.

1. 右小腿回收，右膝屈平，腳尖自然下垂。右前臂外旋，左掌由後向上、向前畫弧下落，右掌掌心翻轉向上，與左掌同時平行落於右膝上方。眼平視前方（圖3-161）。

（1）Draw back the right lower leg and bend the knee levelly, toes naturally hung down. Rotate the right forearm outward, and turn it over to face up. Move the left hand upward and forward in an arc while turning the palm to face up. Both hands fall above the right knee at the same time. Eyes look forward (Figure 3-161).

2. 右腳向前方落下，腳跟著地。兩掌下落，經兩胯旁慢慢握拳。眼看前方（圖3-162）。

（2）Place the right foot on the ground, the heel touching the ground. Both hands fall down by the outside of the hips, while the palms turn into fists slowly. Eyes look forward（Figure 3–162）.

3. 右腳踏實地面，身體重心前移成右弓步。兩拳分別從兩側向上、向前貫出，高與耳齊，兩拳眼斜向下，相距一頭之寬度，兩臂成鉗形狀。眼看前方（圖 3–163）。

（3）Place the entire right foot on the ground solidly. Shift the weight forward to form a right Bow Step. Throw both fists upward and forward from the both sides of the body to punch the opponent's head at ear level, the eyes of the fist facing diagonally down. Eyes look forward（Figure 3–163）.

圖3–161　　圖3–162　　圖3–163

【要點】

在動作中不可低頭弓腰，聳肩揚肘，保持蹬腳時的方向。

Key Points

Do not bow the head or waist; do not lift the shoulders or elbows. Punch in the same direction as the kick.

三十二、左蹬腳

【訣要】

　　摟打著力擊上盤，引他頭上若遮攔；

　　忽然蹬向胸面去，致命方知太極拳；

　　腿稱五行步五行，緩將進退顯屈伸；

　　只因及遠兼敵眾，踢在兩肋蹬在胸。

32. Kicking with the Left Heel

Highlight

Protect your own knees and strike his upper body.

When he uses his hands to parry,

kick his chest.

Step forward or backward slowly

and kick his ribs and chest.

This movement is used to fight

a farer or more enemies.

1. 身體重心向後移動，右腳尖蹺起，稍向外擺。兩拳變掌向左右同時分開，掌心均向外。眼看左掌（圖3-164）。

（1）Shift the weight backward. Lift the toes of the right foot up and turn them a little bit outward. Change the two fists into open palms and separate them to the opposite sides at the same time, palms facing outward. Eyes look at the left hand (Figure 3-164).

2. 身體重心向前移動，隨即將左腳收於右腳內側，腳尖點地，腰順勢先向右再向左擰轉。同時，兩掌分別從左、右側向下、向內畫弧，在胸前交叉抱成斜十字形。左掌在外，右掌在內，掌心均向內。眼看左前方（圖3-165）。

圖3-164　　圖3-165　　圖3-166

（2）Shift the weight forward. Place the left foot close to the right foot, toes touching the ground. Accordingly, twist the waist to the right and then to the left. Meanwhile, draw the two hands in arcs downward and inward from the sides of the body and form an "X" in front of the chest. The left palm is on the outside and the right palm inside, both palms facing inward. Eyes look to the left front（Figure 3–165）.

3. 右腿微屈站穩，左膝提起，左腳向左前方慢慢蹬出，腿尖回勾，力在腳跟。兩掌向左前和右後方同時畫弧撐開，肘部微屈，腕與肩平，左臂左腿上下相對。眼看左掌（圖3–166）。

（3）With the knee slightly bent, the right foot stands stably. Lift the left knee and kick slowly to the left front and deliver the force in the heel. Move the two hands in arcs to the left front and the right back and stop when the wrists are at shoulder level, elbows slightly bent. The left arm is aligned with the left leg vertically. Eyes look at the left hand（Figure 3–166）.

【要點】

同右蹬腳，唯左右相反。

Key Points

This is the same as movement 30, but in the opposite direction.

三十三、掩手肱拳

【訣要】

摟膝最為防下盤，撥開左右即攻前；

決然毒狠還要快，指著敵丹一命亡；

任他鐵壁與銅牆，如開強弓莫慌張；

提拳直指丹田去，教他頃刻命離陽。

33. Hidden Punch

Highlight

Brush over the knees to protect the lower body.

Block off the attack.

Strike his abdomen powerfully

and quickly with no fear.

No matter how strong he is,

such a strike will knock him out.

1. 左腳收回，落於右腳內側，腳尖點地，上體微向右擰轉。兩掌由兩側向上、向內畫弧，舉於面前，兩掌心均向內。眼看前方（圖3-167）。

（1）Draw back the left foot and place it close to the right foot, the toes touching the ground. Turn the upper body to the right slightly. The two hands draw arcs upward and inward from either side of the body, and stop in front of the face, palms facing inward. Eyes look forward (Figure 3–167).

2. 左腳向左前方邁出一步，腳跟著地，上體向右擰轉。兩臂外旋，同時向懷中掩裹，右手下落至右腰間，右掌變拳，左右掌心均向下。眼看右前方（圖3–168a、圖3–168b）。

(2) The left foot takes a step to the left front, heel touching the ground. Turn the upper body to the right. Rotate the arms outward and draw them back in front of the chest. When the right hand passes the right part of the waist, it turns into a fist. Both palms face down. Eyes look to right front(Figure 3–168a,

圖3–167　　　　圖3–168a　　　　圖3–168b

Figure 3–168b）.

3. 上體向左擰轉，身體重心向左移動，左腿前弓，右腿蹬展，成左弓步。左掌隨腰部左轉之勢，握拳收至左腰間，拳心向上；右拳隨上體左轉之勢，向前直臂摻出，也可快速彈擊，拳高與腹平，拳眼向左，拳面斜向前下。眼看右拳（圖3–169）。

（3）Turn the upper body to the left. Shift the weight to the left. Bend the left leg and extend the right leg to form a left Bow Step. With the waist turning to the left, change the left hand into a fist and draw it back to the left waist, palm facing up. Following the turn of the waist, the right fist punches forward straightly and quickly at the level of the abdomen, the eye of the fist pointing to the left. Eyes look at the right hand（Figure 3–169）.

圖3–169

【要點】

摻拳後要鬆肩、垂肘、順肩。如果採取快速發力練法，要注意周身整體腰腿發力，前臂彈抖勁要快速鬆展，拳高不過肩，前後銜接，圓活自然，氣勢貫穿。

Key Points

When punching, pay attention to gathering the force from the waist, leg and the whole body. After punch, relax the shoulders and sink the elbows and shoulders. Keep the entire movement smooth, natural and powerful.

三十四、海底針

【訣要】

直刺鳩尾與中脘，忽下海底勢不偏；
倘逢敵手擒拿下，往下回撤立圓擊；
左手摟按與推施，貼身刺準神貫指；
蓄勢蹲身能聚勁，弓開箭去滿天紅。

34. Needle to the Sea Bottom

Highlight

Pierce toward Jiu Wei Xue and Zhong Wan Xue,

as if a needle down to the sea.

If your hand is being grasped,

withdraw and move it downward,

seeking opportunity to pay back.

Use the left hand to brush, press and push;

use the right hand to thrust

with force through the fingertips.

Lower the body to accumulate power;

thrust the hand like an arrow from a bow.

Note: Jiu Wei Xue is an acupuncture point, which is located in the middle of the chest and the stomach. Zhong Wan Xue is an acupuncture point, which is located in the middle of the Jiu Wei Xue and the navel.

1. 右腳跟進半步，在左腳後側方落下，前腳掌先著地，然後全腳踏實地面；上體向右擰轉身體，重心向後移至右腿，左腳輕輕提起。左拳變掌，掌心向下、向左、向前畫平弧；右拳變側掌下落，經上體右側向上提至右耳旁。眼看前方（圖3-170、圖3-171）。

（1）The right foot takes a half step and falls behind the left foot; the ball of the foot touches the ground first, and then put the entire foot on the ground solidly. Twist the upper body to the right. Shift the weight backward onto the right leg and lift the left foot lightly. The left fist turns into an open palm, palm facing down, and draws an arc leftward and forward. The right fist turns into an open palm, fingers pointing up, palm facing inward, and falls down first, and then rises along the right side of the upper body to the right ear. Eyes look forward (Figure 3-170, Figure 3-171).

2. 上體向左擰轉，右掌從耳側向前下方插掌，指尖斜向前下，掌心向左；左掌向左畫弧按於左胯旁，掌指向前。左腳向前移出半步，腳前掌著地成左虛步。沉肩，塌腰，眼看前下方（圖3-172）。

（2）Twist the upper body to the left. Thrust the right hand towards the lower front from the outside of the ear, fingertips pointing diagonally to the lower front, palm facing the left. Draw the left hand in an arc to the left and press it down by the left

圖3-170　　　　圖3-171　　　　圖3-172

hip, fingers pointing forward. Move the left foot a half step forward with the ball of the foot touching the ground to form a left Empty Step. Sink the shoulders and waists. Eyes look to the lower front (Figure 3–172).

【要點】

跟步和坐腿時，要配合腰部自然旋轉。定勢時，右肩前順，上體可稍向前傾。

Key Points

When the right foot takes a half step backward, cooperate with the waist. Once the posture is settled, push the right shoulder and lean the upper body forward slightly.

三十五、閃通臂

【訣要】

右臂滾提向上托，左掌趁勢進前發；

丁八弓箭看步下，類似猛虎出柵押。

35. Flashing the Arm

Highlight

Rotate and lift the right arm;

push the left hand forward.

Take a step forward,

like a tiger leaping over a barrier.

1. 上體微向右擰轉，左腿提起。兩掌向上提起，左掌指靠近右腕內側。眼看正前方（圖3–173）。

（1）Twist the upper body to the right slightly. Lift the left leg. Raise both hands and place the left palm close to the right wrist. Eyes look forward (Figure 3–173).

2. 左腳向前落地，身體重心前移成左弓步。右掌經面前翻掌上撐停於右額旁，掌心斜向上，指尖向左；左掌自胸前向前推出，掌心向前，高與鼻平。眼看左掌（圖3–174）。

（2）The left foot falls ahead of the body. Shift the weight forward to form a left Bow Step. The right hand turns over in

圖3–173　　　　　　　　圖3–174

front of the face and pushes up to the right side of the forehead, palm facing diagonally up, fingers pointing to the left. The left hand pushes forward in front of the chest, palm facing forward at the nose level. Eyes look at the left palm (Figure 3–174).

【要點】

提手時，不要聳肩吊肘。定式時，要向前、向下鬆腰，右胯不要外撇。

Key Points

When raising the hands, do not lift the shoulders and elbows. When the posture is settled, relax the waist. Do not push the right hip out.

三十六、右左分腳

【訣要】

撤步雙捋敵勁空，分手使腳勢須平；
後腿微屈亦蓄勢，須掛手掤脊須中；
五行步內此為雄，進退左右變無窮；
縱然用腳分踢去，高在鼻梁低在胸。

36. Separate Feet

Highlight

Step backward and pull the enemy

with both hands.

Keep balance while separating the hands and kicking.

Bend the back leg slightly to store power.

This is the strongest in Five Footworks in Tai Chi.

Move forward or backward with unlimited changes.

Kick on the enemy's nose or chest.

Note: Five Footworks are: Forward Step, Backward Step, Left Step, Right Step, and Central and Balance Yourself.

1. 身體重心向後移動，左腳尖儘量向內扣回，上體向右後擰轉。兩掌向兩側畫弧撐開，掌心均向外。眼看右前方（圖3-175）。

（1）Shift the weight backward. Swing the toes of the left

圖3-175　　　　圖3-176a　　　　圖3-176b

foot inward as much as possible. Turn the upper body to the right back. Separate the hands in arcs in opposite directions, palms facing outward. Eyes look to right front (Figure 3–175).

2. 身體重心向左移動；同時，收右腳至左腳內側，腳尖點地。兩手向下再向體前畫弧，在腹前交叉後再合抱於胸前成斜十字形，右掌在外，左掌在內，兩掌心均向內。眼看右前方（圖3–176a、圖3–176b）。

(2) Shift the weight to the left. Meanwhile, move the right foot close to the left foot, toes touching the ground. Both hands draw arcs downward and forward, and past the abdomen to form an "X" in front of the chest. The right hand is on the outside and the left hand is inside, palms facing inward. Eyes look to right front(Figure 3–176a, Figure 3–176b).

3. 左腿微屈站穩，右腿屈膝提起，右腳向右前方慢慢踢出，腳面展平。兩掌同時向右前方和左後方畫弧撐開，掌心均向外，腕高與肩平，雙肘微屈，右臂與右腿上下相對。眼看右掌（圖3–177）。

(3) The left leg bends slightly and stands stably. With the knee bent, lift the right foot up and kick to the right front slowly, the foot stretched. At the same time, separate the hands in arcs, the right hand to the right front and the left to the left

back, palms facing outward, elbows bent slightly and wrists at the shoulder level. The right arm is aligned with the right leg vertically. Eyes look at the right hand (Figure 3–177).

4. 右小腿屈收，右腳向右前方落地，腳跟著地。右前臂外旋，右掌心轉向上並稍向內收；左掌下落經左腰側向前、向上畫弧並從右前臂上方穿出，掌心向前。眼看右掌（圖3–178）。

(4) Draw back the right lower leg and land the foot on the ground in the right front, heel touching the ground. Rotate the right forearm outward and draw the hand back slightly while turning the palm over to face up. The left hand falls down by the left side of the waist and draws an arc forward and upward over the right forearm, palm facing forward. Eyes look at the

圖3–177　　　　　圖3–178

right hand（Figure 3-178）.

5. 右腳踏實地面，身體重心向前移動，左腿伸直。左掌向上、向前畫弧，掌心向下；右掌向下、向後畫弧，掌心向上。眼看左掌（圖3-179）。

（5）Place the right foot on the ground. Shift the weight forward. Extend the left leg. The left hand draws an arc upward and forward, palm facing down. The right hand draws an arc downward and backward, palm facing up. Eyes look at the left hand（Figure 3-179）.

6. 左腳收至右腳內側，腳尖點地，腰先向右再向左旋轉。左掌向下，右掌向上，同時繼續畫圓，至胸前時，兩掌腕部交叉合抱成斜十字形，左掌在外，右

圖3-179

掌在內，掌心均向內。眼看左前方（圖3–180）。

（6）Place the left foot beside the right foot, toes touching the ground. Turn the waist to the right and then to the left. Move the left hand downward and the right hand upward. Both hands stop in front of the chest to form an "X". The left hand is on the outside, and the right hand is on the inside, palms facing inward. Eyes look to the left front (Figure 3–180).

7. 右腿微屈站穩，左腿屈膝提起，左腳向左前方慢慢踢出，腳面伸平。兩掌同時向左前和右後方畫弧撐開，掌心均向外，腕高與肩平，兩肘部微屈，左臂與左腿上下相對。眼看左掌（圖3–181）。

（7）The right leg bends slightly and stands steadily. Lift the left leg with the knee bent, and kick to the left front slowly,

圖3–180　　　　　　　　圖3–181

the back of the foot stretched. Separate the hands in arcs, the left hand to the left front and the right to the right back, palms facing outward, elbows bent slightly and wrists at the shoulder level. The left arm is aligned with the left leg vertically. Eyes look at the left hand (Figure 3–181).

【要點】

撐身、換勢、撐掌、踢腿要協調一致，上下相隨。

Key Points

Twisting the body, changing the postures, opening the hands, and kicking are all coordinated and seamless.

三十七、摟膝打掌

【訣要】

起肩過胯膝到摟，指點掌印蓋當頭；
眉間一聲霹靂震，小丑天魔亦罷休；
肘部須防敵暗推，連環摟打任施為；
任他強硬如山岳，肩頭一掌或鳩尾。

37. One Hand Blocks and the Another Strikes

Highlight

Move a hand from the shoulder, by the hip,
around the knee and then over the head.

48式養生太極拳

Move another hand to attack the enemy's forehead;

even devils are scared away.

Protect yourself with the elbows

and attack continuously.

No matter how strong an opponent is,

he will be beaten by the strike on his shoulder or tailbone.

1. 左小腿屈收，左腳落於右腳內側，上體向右擰轉。右掌翻轉上舉，高與頭平；左掌隨轉體動作向上、向右畫弧落於右肩前，掌心向下。眼看右掌（圖3-182）。

（1）Withdraw the left leg and put the foot beside the right foot. Turn the upper body to the right. Turn over the right hand and raise it up to head level. While the body turns, the left hand draws an arc upward and rightward, and stops in front of the right shoulder, palm facing down. Eyes look at the right hand (Figure 3-182).

2. 上體向左擰轉，左腳向前邁出一步，身體重心移於左腿成左弓步。左掌下落經左膝前摟過，按於左胯旁，掌心向下，掌指向前；右掌屈收經右耳側向前推出，掌心向前，高與鼻平。眼看右掌（圖3-183）。

（2）Twist the upper body to the left. The left foot takes a

step forward. Shift the weight onto the left leg to form a left Bow Step. The left hand falls down, moves around the left knee and presses down by the side of the left hip, palm facing downward, fingers pointing forward. Draw back the right hand and push it forward from the outside of the ear, palm facing forward at nose level. Eyes look at the right hand (Figure 3-183).

3. 身體重心向後移動，左腳尖蹺起外展。上體向左擰轉。兩臂外旋，右掌心轉向左，左掌心轉向上。眼看右掌（圖3-184）。

(3) Shift the weight backward. Tilt the toes of the left foot and swing them outward. Twist the upper body to the left. Rotate both arms outward, the right palm facing the left, the left palm facing up. Eyes look at the right hand (Figure 3-184).

圖3-182　　圖3-183　　　　圖3-184

4. 左腳踏實地面，右腳提起向前上步，做右摟膝打掌，動作同左式，唯左右方向相反（圖3-185、圖3-186）。

(4) Place the left foot on the ground solidly. The right foot lifts up and step forward. Repeat the above movements in the opposite direction (Figure 3-185, Figure 3-186).

【要點】

推掌時，肩略向前順，鬆腰，沉肩，上體保持正直，轉換動作要協調一致。

Key Points

When pushing the hand forward, push the shoulder forward slightly. Sink the shoulders, relax the waist and keep the upper body upright. Coordinate the movements with each other.

圖3-185　　　　　圖3-186

三十八、上步擒打

【訣要】

舉動輕靈神內斂，莫教斷續一氣研；

左右宜有虛實處，意上寓下後天還；

頂頂貫頂兩膀鬆，採挒下氣把襠撐；

右将左擒須交手，忽隱忽現進則長。

38. Step Forward and Grasp the Enemy

Highlight

Move lightly and seamlessly with the mind focused.

Move to the right or left with a solid or empty step.

When you focus on the upper body,

do not forget the lower;

when you focus on the front,

do not forget the back.

Draw the head up and relax the shoulders.

If the enemy try to pull you,

arch your crotch and lower your body.

Crossing the hands,

pull with the right hand and grasp with the left.

Show or hide the hands to create more advantages.

1.身體重心向後移動，右腳尖蹺起，並向右外展。左掌翻轉向上並微向後收，右掌屈肘從左前臂上向前穿出，掌心斜向外。眼看前方（圖3-187）。

（1）Shift the weight backward. Tilt the toes of the right foot up and swing them outward. Turn the left palm upward and draw it backward slightly. Bend the right elbow and thrust the hand forward over the left forearm, palm facing diagonally outward. Eyes look forward (Figure 3–187).

2.右腳落實地面，身體重心向前移動，身體向右擰轉。右掌自左前方向右抹掌畫弧，左掌向左、向後畫弧，收於腹前。眼看右掌（圖3-188）。

（2）Plant the right foot on the ground solidly. Shift the weight forward and twist the body to the right. The right hand

圖3-187　　　圖3-188　　　圖3-189

draws an arc from the left front to the right. The left hand draws an arc leftward and backward, and stops in front of the abdomen. Eyes look at the right hand (Figure 3–188).

3. 左腳提起向前上一步。右掌向外畫弧，再握拳收於右腰間，拳心向上；左掌向左、再向前畫弧，扣腕握拳停於體前，拳心向下，拳眼斜向內，高與肩平。眼看左拳（圖3-189）。

（3）The left foot takes a step forward. The right hand moves outward in an arc, and then turns into a fist at the right side of the waist, palm facing up. The left hand moves leftward and then forward in an arc; the wrist turns inward and the palm turns into a fist in front of the body, palm facing down, and the eye of the fist pointing diagonally inward at the shoulder level. Eyes look at the left hand (Figure 3–189).

4. 左腳落實地面，身體重心向前移動成左弓步。右拳自腰間向前從左腕上部打出，拳眼向上，高與肩平；左拳微向後撤，收停於右腕下方，拳心向下。眼看右拳（圖3-190）。

（4）Plant the left foot on the ground solidly. Shift the weight forward to form a left Bow Step. The right fist punches forward from the waist over the left wrist, the eye of the fist pointing up at the shoulder level. Draw back the left fist slightly and stop it under the right wrist, palm facing down. Eyes look at the right hand (Figure 3-190).

【要點】

穿掌外抹接兩掌畫弧要連貫圓活。腰部先向右擰轉，再向左擰轉，將右拳打出。

Key Points

Move the hands smoothly and seamlessly. Turn the waist to the right first, then to the left, and then pouch.

三十九、如封似閉

【訣要】

如封似閉更出奇，採挒肘靠四般施；

圖3-190　　　　　　　圖3-191

不怕他家用猛力，開弓發箭總相宜；

雙推雙撲勢更凶，好似猛虎入羊群；

緊防剛勁剎不住，偶然過量即成空。

39. As if Blocking and Shutting

Highlight

This movement is amazing,

with grabbing, tearing and pushing.

No matter how hard he fights,

you always can find a chance to beat him.

Push or pounce with both hands,

powerful like a tiger into a herd of sheep.

Do not forget to save some power;

overusing it will cause the attack to fail.

1. 右腳跟進半步，前腳掌著地。同時，兩拳變掌，掌心斜向上。眼向前平視（圖3–191）。

（1）The right foot takes a half step forward, the ball of the foot touching the ground. At the same time, both fists become palms, palms facing diagonally up. Eyes look straightly forward (Figure 3–191).

2. 身體重心後移，右腳隨即落實地面，左腳提起向前上半步，左腿屈膝成左弓步。兩掌緩緩分開收至胸前，與兩肩同寬；同時，兩前臂邊收邊向內旋，掌心翻轉向前，兩掌下落經腹前再向前按出，掌心向前，兩腕高與肩平。眼看正前方（圖3-192～圖3-194）。

（2）Shift the weight backward. Place the right foot on the ground. The left foot lifts up and takes a half step forward, with the knee bent, to form a left Bow Step. Slowly separate the hands at the width of the shoulders in front of the chest. Meanwhile, draw the forearms back while rotating them inward and turning the palms forward. When both hands fall down to the abdomen, push them forward, palms facing forward, wrists at shoulder level. Eyes look forward（Figure 3-192～Figure 3-194）.

圖3-192　　　　圖3-193　　　　圖3-194

【要點】

兩掌向後收回時，要邊收邊分邊翻轉，並向兩肘牽引。肘部不要停頓，前臂揚起向後捲收。身體重心移動要虛實分明。按掌和弓腿要協調一致，同時到達終點。

Key Points

Synchronize the movements of drawing the hands back, separating them, and turning them over, led by the elbows. Without pause, lift the forearms and roll them back. Shift the weight clearly. Pressing down the palms and bending the legs are coordinated and completed at the same time.

四十、左雲手

【訣要】

提掛掤擲滾按推，全憑脊骨圓轉隨；

雲到敵人雙肋後，銅牆鐵柱一起推。

40. Left Cloud Hand

Highlight

Lifting, blocking, pushing, throwing

and rolling all depend on a strong spine and the back.

When the hands move to the enemy's ribs,

push him forcefully.

　　1. 身體重心向後移動，左腳尖向內回扣，上體向右擰轉。右掌自左向右經面前畫立圓，掌心向內；左掌自左經腹前向右畫立圓，掌心由外向內。上體及視線隨右手轉動（圖3-195）。

　　（1）Shift the weight backward. Swing the toes of the left foot inward. Twist the upper body to the right. The right hand moves upward, rightward and then downward to draw a vertical circle, past the face, palm facing inward. The left hand moves downward, rightward and then upward to draw a vertical circle, past the abdomen and turns the palm to face inward. The upper body and eyes follow the right hand (Figure 3-195).

　　2. 上體向左擰轉，身體重心移至左腿，右腳收於左腳內側，兩腳相距10～20公分，兩腳尖向前。同時，左掌掌心向內，自右經面前向左立圓雲轉，至身體左側時翻掌心向外；右掌自右經腹前向左立圓雲轉，掌心外轉向內。上體及視線均隨左掌轉動（圖3-196、圖3-197）。

　　（2）Twist the upper body to the left and shift the weight onto the left leg. Place the right foot beside the left foot, 10～20 cm apart, toes pointing forward. Meanwhile, move the left hand in a circle to the left in front of the face and turn the palm facing outward when it reaches the left side of the body. The right hand draws a circle from the right to the left in front of the abdomen, palm turning to face inward. The upper body and eyes follow the left hand (Figure 3–196, Figure 3–197).

3. 上體向右擰轉，身體重心移向右腿，左腳向左側跨出一步，兩腳尖均向前。右掌經面前向右立圓雲轉，左掌經腹前向右立圓雲轉，雲轉至右側時，兩掌逐漸翻轉。上體及視線隨右掌轉動（圖3–198、圖3–199）。

（3）Twist the upper body to the right. Shift the weight onto the right leg. The left foot takes a step to the left, toes pointing forward. The right hand draws a circle to the right in front of the face. The left hand draws a circle in front of abdomen. When moving the hands to the right side of the body, turn the

圖3–195　　　圖3–196　　　圖3–197

palms over. The upper body and eyes follow the right hand (Figure 3-198, Figure 3-199).

4. 上體向左擰轉，身體重心移至左腿，右腳收於左腳內側，兩腳相距10～20公分，腳尖均向前。同時，左掌經面前向左立圓雲轉，右掌經腹前向左立圓雲轉，雲轉至身體左側時，左掌心轉向外，右掌心轉向內。上體及視線隨左掌轉動（圖3-200、圖3-201）。

(4) Twist the upper body to the left. Shift the weight onto the left leg. Place the right foot beside the left foot, 10～20 cm apart, toes pointing forward. Meanwhile, the left hand draws a circle to the left in front of the face. The right hand draws a circle to the left in front of abdomen. When the hands move to the left side of the body, the left palm turns to face outward, and the

圖3-198　　　　　圖3-199

right palm turns to face inward. The upper body and the eyes follow the left hand（Figure 3-200, Figure 3-201）.

5. 上述動作再重複一次，唯最後收併右腿時，右腳要向內扣回約45°（圖3-202～圖3-205）。

（5）Repeat the above movement, then draw back the right

圖3-200   圖3-201   圖3-202

圖3-203   圖3-204   圖3-205

leg, turn the right foot inward about 45° (Figure 3–202～Figure 3–205).

【要點】

整體動作要求同右雲手，唯方向向左。當第三次收右步時，注意內扣右腳，以便轉換下個動作。

Key Points

The same as those in 27 The Right Cloud Hand in an opposite direction. When the movement is done, turn the right foot inward to prepare for the next movement.

四十一、右撇身捶

【訣要】

右腕忽為順手執，回肘掄臂包左肋；
左手扣緊休鬆勁，肋下交叉是此勢；
撇身扣疊勢為雄，引進敵來更落空；
撇身反背一拳去，尚留左掌未前伸；
轉身壓腕破擒拿，眉前一掌見紅花；
敵來扣腿兼撲面，移步掤推前跌他。

41. Throw the Right Fist

Highlight

Get the right wrist ready.

Swing the left arm

and draw back the elbow to cover the ribs.

Continue to move the left hand

to cross the right hand under the ribs.

If the enemy pounces on you, retreat fast;

he will fall through.

Throw the left fist at him;

save the right hand to guard yourself.

Turn the body and press the wrist against being caught;

punch his forehead.

Trip him with a leg and strike his face;

step up, pulling and pushing to make him fall over.

1. 身體重心移於右腿，左腳向身後撤一步，右腿屈膝成右弓步。左掌翻轉使掌心向上、向體前畫弧回收至腹前，右掌翻轉使掌心向前下，經左前臂上方向前伸探，停於體前，高與肩平。眼看右掌（圖3-206）。

（1）Shift the weight onto the right leg. The left foot takes a step backward. Bend the right knee to form a right Bow Step. The left hand turns over to face up, draws an arc forward, and stops in front of the abdomen. The right hand turns over to face down, extends forward over the left forearm and stops at shoulder level in front of the body. Eyes look at the right hand (Figure 3-206).

2. 身體重心移於左腿，右腳收至左腳內側，腳尖點地，上體向左擰轉。右掌下落變拳收於小腹前，拳心向內，拳眼向左；左掌向左、向上再向體前畫弧，翻掌心向下，附於右前臂內側。頭隨身轉，目視前方（圖3-207）。

（2）Shift the weight onto the left leg. Move the right foot close to the left foot, toes touching the ground. Twist the upper body to the left. The right hand becomes a fist falling down to the abdomen, palm facing inward, the eye of the fist facing the left. The left hand draws an arc leftward, upward and forward, and rests on the right forearm, palm facing down. The head follows the body. Eyes look forward（Figure 3-207）.

3. 身體微向右擰轉，右腳向右前方邁出一步，身

圖3-206　　　　圖3-207　　　　圖3-208

體重心隨即前移於右腿，右腿屈膝，左腿伸直，成右弓步。右拳上提經左胸前向前、向上撇出，拳心斜向上，高與肩平，左掌附於右前臂內側一起向前撇出。眼看右拳（圖3–208）。

(3) Twist the body to the right slightly. Move the right foot a step to the right front. Shift the weight onto the right leg. Bend the right knee and extend the left leg to form a right Bow Step. Raise the right fist in front of the left chest and throw it forward and upward, palm facing diagonally up at shoulder level. The left palm, which rests on the right forearm, follows the right fist. Eyes look at the right hand (Figure 3–208).

【要點】

撇出時，步型成右弓步。兩腿不要歪擰、交錯，動作要上下協調一致。

Key Points

When throwing the fist, the feet form a right Bow Step. Do not twist or cross the legs. The upper body and lower body are coordinated.

四十二、玉女穿梭

【訣要】

上盤右手用掤肘，左臂斜穿肘後擠；

貼手滾擠才得機，按手化勁轉身遠；

順他來勁手纏前，左纏右兼掤進步；

梭要輕靈玉女穿，雙將敵臂採還捯；

如鷹搏兔要神速，隨他抽撤忙進步；

順手來掤拗手擊，順勁推掤敵更偏。

42. Working with a Shuttle

Highlight

Use the right hand to push the enemy's upper body.

Thrust the left arm and the elbow backward.

Roll the enemy's hands down

and get a chance to strike him.

Press his hand and lead his way.

Comply with his power and twist forward;

Push and step up,

just like a maid playing a shuttle with a great skill.

When he withdraws,

move forward as quickly as an eagle capturing a rabbit.

If he defends with his hand,

rotate it and push him away.

1. 身體重心向後移動，右腳尖蹺起向內回扣，上體稍向左擰轉。左掌自右前臂上穿出，掌心斜向下；右拳同時變掌，微向後收，掌心斜向上（圖3-209）。

（1）Shift the weight backward. Tilt the toes of the right foot up and turn it inward. Twist the upper body to the left slightly. Thrust the left hand over the right forearm, palm facing diagonally down. Turn the right fist into an open palm and draw it backward slightly, palm facing diagonally up（Figure 3–209）.

2. 上體再稍向左擰轉，右腳落實地面，身體重心移至右腿。左掌向左前方抹掌，右掌收於左肘內側下方，兩掌心上下斜相對。眼看左掌（圖3–210）。

（2）Continue to twist the upper body to the left. Place the right foot on the ground. Shift the weight onto the right leg. Move the left hand toward the left front and draw the right hand back by the left elbow, palms facing diagonally to each other. Eyes look at the left hand（Figure 3–210）.

圖3–209　　　　　　　圖3–210

3. 上體向右擰轉，兩掌自前方向下捋回，右掌捋至右胯旁，掌心向上；左掌捋至腹前，掌心斜向下。同時，左腳收至右腳內側。眼看右前方（圖3-211）。

（3）Twist the upper body to the right. Pull both hands from the front downward and stop the right hand in front of the right hip, palm facing up; stop the left hand in front of the abdomen, palm facing diagonally down. At the same time, move the left foot close to the right foot. Eyes look forward (Figure 3-211).

4. 左腳向左前方邁出一步，身體重心向前移至左腿，成左弓步。左前臂外旋，右前臂內旋，兩掌上提至胸前，右掌指輕附於左腕內側，隨身體重心向前移動之勢自右向前畫平圓，左掌心斜向上，右掌心斜向下，高與肩平。眼看左掌（圖3-212）。

圖3-211　　　　圖3-212　　　　圖3-213

（4）The left foot takes a step to the left front. Shift the weight forward onto the left leg to form a left Bow Step. Rotate the left forearm outward and the right forearm inward, both hands by the chest. Rest the right palm at the inner side of the left wrist. With the weight shifted forward, move both hands in a flat circle forward, the left palm facing diagonally up, and the right palm facing diagonally down at shoulder level. Eyes look at the left hand (Figure 3-212).

5. 上體向左擰轉，左臂屈肘，左掌向左、向後畫平圓，掌心斜向上，右掌仍附於左腕內側。右腳同時向前跟進半步，腳前掌著地。眼看左掌（圖3-213）。

（5）Twist the upper body to the left. Bend the left elbow and move the left hand in a circle leftward and backward, palm facing diagonally up. The right hand still remains at the inner side of the left wrist. Meanwhile, the right foot follows a half step forward, the ball of the foot touching the ground. Eyes look at the left hand (Figure 3-213).

6. 右腳落實地面，身體重心移至右腿，左腳提起，上體向右擰轉。右掌自左前臂內側收於胸前，左前臂內旋，左掌翻轉使掌心斜向前。眼看右前方（圖

3-214）。

（6）Place the right foot on the ground. Shift the weight onto the right leg. Lift the left foot. Twist the upper body to the right. Draw the right hand from the left forearm back in front of the chest. Rotate the left forearm inward and turn the palm over to face diagonally forward. Eyes look to the right front（Figure 3-214）.

7. 左腳向前邁出一步，左腿屈膝成左弓步，上體向左擰轉。左掌上架於左額前上方，掌心斜向上；右掌向前推出，掌心向前，掌指斜向上，高與鼻平。眼看右掌（圖3-215）。

（7）Move the left foot a step forward and bend the left leg to form a left Bow Step. Twist the upper body to the left. Push the left hand up and stop it at the upper left front of the forehead,

圖3-214　　　　圖3-215　　　　圖3-216

palm facing diagonally up. Push the right hand forward, palm facing forward, fingers pointing up at nose level. Eyes look at the right hand（3–215）.

8. 身體重心向後移動，左腳尖蹺起內扣，上體向右擰轉。左臂外旋使掌心斜向上，落於體前；右掌稍回收，再從左前臂上穿出（圖3–216）。

（8）Shift the weight backward. Tilt the toes of the left foot up and turn them inward. Twist the upper body to the right. Rotate the left arm so that the palm faces diagonally up in front of the body. Draw back the right hand slightly and thrust it over the left forearm（Figure 3–216）.

9. 左腳落實地面，身體重心移於左腿，上體稍向右擰轉。右掌向右前方抹掌，左掌收於右肘內側下方，兩掌心斜相對。眼看右掌（圖3–217）。

（9）Place the left foot on the ground. Shift the weight onto the left leg. Turn the upper body to the right slightly. Move the right hand toward the right front and draw the left hand back by the right elbow, palms facing each other. Eyes look at the right hand（Figure 3–217）.

10. 上體向左擰轉，兩掌自前向下捋回，左掌捋至左胯旁，掌心向上；右掌捋至腹前，掌心斜向下。同時，右腳收於左腳內側。眼看左前方（圖3–218）。

（10）Twist the upper body to the left. Pull the two hands downward and stop the left hand in front of the left hip, palm facing up; stop the right hand in front of the abdomen, palm facing diagonally down. At the same time, move the right foot close to the left foot. Eyes look forward (Figure 3–218).

11. 右腳向右前方邁出一步，身體重心前移成右弓步。兩前臂旋轉，兩掌向上收至胸前，左掌指輕附於右腕內側，隨重心前移自左向前畫平圓，右掌心斜向上，左掌心斜向下，高與肩平。眼看右掌（圖3–219）。

（11）The right foot takes a step to the right front. Shift the weight forward to form a right Bow Step. Rotate both forearms

圖3–217　　　　　　圖3–218

and raise the hands up to the chest. Rest the left palm lightly at the inner side of the right wrist, which draws a flat circle forward at shoulder level, the right palm facing diagonally up, the left palm facing diagonally down, and the weight shifted forward. Eyes look at the right hand (Figure 3–219).

12. 上體向右擰轉，左腳向前跟進半步，腳前掌著地。右臂屈肘向右、向後畫平圓，左掌仍附於右腕內側。眼看右掌（圖3–220）。

（12）Twist the upper body to the right. The left foot follows a half step forward, the ball of the foot touching the ground. Bend the right elbow and draw a flat circle rightward and backward. The left palm is still attached to the inner side of the right wrist. Eyes look at the right hand (Figure 3–220).

圖3–219　　　　　　　　圖3–220

13. 左腳落實地面，身體重心移至左腿，右腳輕提，上體向左擰轉。左掌收於胸前，右前臂內旋，右掌心斜向前。眼看右前方（圖3-221）。

（13）Place the left foot on the ground. Shift the weight onto the left leg. Lift the right foot up gently and twist the upper body to the left. Move the left hand back and stop it in front of the chest. Rotate the right forearm inward, palm facing diagonally forward. Eyes look to the right front (Figure 3–221).

14. 右腳向前邁出一步，右腿屈膝成右弓步，上體向右擰轉。右掌上架於右額前上方，掌心斜向上；左掌向前推出，高與鼻平，掌心向前。眼看左掌（圖3-222）。

（14）Move the right foot a step forward and bend the right leg to form a right Bow Step. Twist the upper body to the right. Push the right hand up to the right front of the forehead, palm facing diagonally up. Push the left hand forward, palm facing forward at nose level. Eyes look at the left hand (Figure 3– 222).

【要點】

手腳配合動作要協調，做到：扣腳和穿掌一致，弓腿和抹掌一致，下捋和收腳一致，翻掌向前畫平圓與上步弓腿一致，向後畫平圓和跟步一致，翻掌和後坐一致，前推、上架和上步弓腿一致。上體要直，胯要正。防止吊肘、歪身、扭胯。

Key Points

The movement of feet is coordinated with that of hands, such as turning the toes with thrusting the hand, bending the leg with moving the hands, drawing back the foot with pulling back the hand, stepping forward and bending leg with turning over the palm and drawing a circle, following a step forward with drawing a backward circle, overturning the palm with moving the body backward, and stepping forward to form a Bow Step with pushing the hands up and forward. Keep the upper body and the hips upright. Do not lift the elbows, lean the body or twist the hips.

圖3-221　　　　　　　圖3-222

四十三、退步穿掌

【訣要】

穿掌原似地頭蛇，如似一蝶下尋花；

雙捋半捌開半岔，後路窮時用不差。

43. Step Backward and Thrust the Hand

Highlight

Crouch down like a snake,

or like a butterfly seeking a flower.

Lower the body, pull, and tear;

this can also be used for an escape.

1. 身體重心後移至左腿，右腳尖蹺起，上體向左擰轉。左掌向左、向後畫弧至左腰間，掌心向下；右前臂外旋，右掌落於體前，掌心斜向左。眼看右掌（圖3-223）。

(1) Shift the weight backward onto the left leg. Tilt the toes of the right foot up. Twist the upper body to the left. Draw the left hand leftward and backward to the left waist, palm facing down. Rotate the right forearm and stop the hand in front of the body, palm facing diagonally left. Eyes look at the right hand (Figure 3-223).

2. 右腳提起經左腳內側向後撤步，左腿屈膝成左弓步。右掌下按落於左肘下方，左掌心翻轉向上捲收至腰間，再經右前臂上向前上方穿出，高與眼平。眼看左掌（圖3-224）。

（2）Lift the right foot up and move it backward by the inner side of the left foot. Bend the left leg to form a left Bow Step. Press the right hand down to the position below the left elbow. Turn over the left palm to face up and rotate it back to the waist, and then thrust it over the right forearm to the upper front at the eyes level. Eyes look at the left hand (Figure 3-224).

【要點】

坐腿要充分，收腳要輕靈，退步要穩健，上下要配合，手腳動作要協調。

圖3-223　　　　　　圖3-224

Key Points

Sufficiently shift the weight onto the leg. Withdraw the foot gently and step backward steadily. The upper body and lower body, hands and feet should coordinate in movements.

四十四、虛步壓掌

【訣要】

極柔極剛極虛靈，運若抽絲處處明；

開展緊湊乃縝密，待機而動如貓行。

44. Push Down in Empty Step

Highlight

Extremely soft, light but hard,

as if pulling a thread.

Take an opportunity and move fast like a cat.

1. 身體重心後移，左腳內扣，上體向右後轉。同時，右掌收至腹前，左掌舉於左額上方。眼向前平視（圖3–225）。

（1）Shift the weight backward. Turn the toes of the left foot inward. Turn the upper body backward. At the same time, move the right hand back in front of the abdomen. Lift the left hand up over the left forehead. Eyes look straight forward (Figure

3-225).

2. 身體重心移至左腿，右腳提起，腳尖轉向前成右虛步，上體向下鬆沉，微向前俯。左掌自上而下橫按於右膝上方，掌心向下，拇指向內；右掌按於右胯旁，掌指向前。眼看前方（圖3-226）。

（2）Shift the weight onto the left leg. Lift the right leg and turn the toes forward to form a right Empty Step. Lower and relax the upper body, and lean forward slightly. The left hand presses down over the right knee, palm facing down, thumb pointing inward. The right hand presses down by the right hip, fingers pointing forward. Eyes look forward（Figure 3-226）.

圖3-225　　　　　　圖3-226

【要點】

轉身成虛步時，右腳要稍向右移動，做到鬆腰鬆胯。壓掌時要順肩轉腰，不要低頭彎腰，上體不可過於前俯。

Key Points

When turning the body to form the Empty Step, move the right foot to the right slightly. Relax the waist and hips. When pressing the hand down, push the shoulder forward slightly and turn the waist. Do not lower the head or bend the back. Do not lean forward too much.

四十五、獨立托掌

【訣要】

如是蜇龍升上天，鳳凰展翅立平原；

擎掌上托額仰面，提膝直撞下丹田；

步下連隨分進步，手中擒拿換陰陽；

金雞獨立間堪式，變化擎提最忌偏；

下額帷虛擎掌托，哪堪左右更提膝；

追魂索命休輕用，怕他高眠臥不起。

45. Stand on One Leg to Lift the Hand

Highlight

Like a dragon flying up to the sky

or a phoenix spreading its wings,

raise the palm over the head;

lift the knee to hit the opponent's lower abdomen.

Steps alternate from forward to backward

hile hands change between Yin and Yang.

Stand straight on one leg;

do not lean in any direction.

If the opponent is struck on his chin

with the hand and his abdomen

with the knee at the same time,

he may never rise.

左腳蹬地，左腿微屈站穩，右腿屈膝提起，腳尖自然下垂，成左獨立步。同時，上體左轉，右掌翻轉向上托起，舉於體前，掌心向上，掌指向前，腕與胸平；左掌向左、向上畫弧，撐於體側，高與肩平，掌心向外，掌指斜向前上。眼看右掌（圖3-227）。

The left foot pushes the ground; the leg bends slightly and stands stably. Raise the right leg and bend the knee, toes pointing down naturally to form a left One Leg Stand Step. Meanwhile, turn the upper body to the left. Turn the right hand over and push it upward in front of the body, palm facing up, fingers pointing forward, wrist at chest level. Move the left hand in an arc leftward and upward, and stop it by the side of the body, palm facing outward, fingers pointing diagonally up at shoulder level. Eyes look at the right hand (Figure 3–227).

【要點】

蹬起、轉腰、托掌三者要協調一致。定式時要鬆腰、含胸、沉肩、墜肘、沉腕，隨勢緩緩呼氣，體現出動作的虛實變化。

Key Points

The movements of pushing the ground, turning the body and lifting the hand are coordinated with each other. When posture is settled, relax the waist, draw in the chest, and sink the shoulders, elbows and the wrists. Exhale slowly.

圖3-227

四十六、馬步靠

【訣要】

其法分肩背，斜身勢用肩，肩中還有背；

一旦機會乘，轟然如倒碓，不丟我中心；

百使百成功，姿勢若有偏，失中徒無功。

46. Push with the Shoulder

Highlight

Push the enemy with the shoulder and the back.

Knock him down while keeping yourself balanced.

Otherwise, you will fail for sure.

1. 右腳在體前橫步下落，身體重心移至右腿，上體向右擰轉。右臂內旋，右掌向下、向右畫弧；左臂外旋，左掌向上、向右畫弧。眼向前平視（圖3-228）。

（1）The right foot falls down before the body with toes pointing to the left. Shift the weight onto the right leg. Twist the upper body to the right. Rotate the right arm and move the hand in an arc downward and rightward. Rotate the left arm outward and move the hand in an arc upward and rightward. Eyes look forward (Figure 3-228).

2.左腳收於右腳內側。右掌翻轉向上側舉至右耳側，左掌變拳，落於胸前，拳心向下。眼看前方（圖3-229）。

（2）Move the left foot close to the right foot. Turn the right hand over and lift it to the outside of the right ear. The left palm turns into a fist and falls down by the chest, palm facing down. Eyes look forward (Figure 3-229).

3.左腳向左前方上步，身體重心略向前移成半馬步，上體稍向左轉。左前臂下落經腹前向前靠出，左臂微屈停於身體左側，左拳拳眼向內，拳面向下，停於左膝上方；右掌落於左肘內側，掌心向前，推助左臂向前靠出。眼看左前方（圖3-230）。

（3）Move the left foot a step forward. Shift the weight for-

圖3-228　　　圖3-229　　　　　圖3-230

ward slightly to form a half Horse Step. Turn the upper body to the left slightly. The left forearm falls down to the abdomen. Bend the left arm slightly and push it forward, fist above the left knee and the eye of the fist facing inward. The right hand rests at the inner side of the left elbow and pushes the left arm forward, palm facing forward. Eyes look to the left front (Figure 3–230).

【要點】

上前墊步和上步時都要腳跟先著地，然後隨重心前移全腳踏實。定式時，腰向前、向下鬆沉，保持樁步穩定，上體正直。發力時，要做到用腰腿發力，周身完整一氣，小腹充實，快速整齊。半馬步型，兩腳夾角不要超過90°，重心稍偏於後腿，要圓襠，後膝稍向內合。

Key Points

When stepping forward, the heel touches the ground first, and then, as the weight is shifted forward, place the entire foot on the ground solidly. When the posture settled, relax the waist. Keep the stance stable and the upper body upright. Deliver force to the waist and leg. Unite the whole body together with the lower abdomen solid. In the half Horse Step, the angle between the feet should not be over 90°. The weight is mostly on the back leg, crotch arched and the back knee pushed inward slightly.

四十七、轉身捋掌下勢

【訣要】

下勢原似地頭蛇，如似一蝶下尋花；

雙捋半捌開半岔，後路窮時用不差。

47. Turn and Lower the Body While Pulling Hand

Highlight

Crouch down like a snake,

or like a butterfly seeking a flower.

Lower the body, pull, and tear;

this can also be used for an escape.

1. 身體重心後移，上體微向右轉，左腳尖外展。左拳變掌，兩掌掌心同時轉向右並微向後收。眼看前方（圖3-231）。

（1）Shift the weight backward. Turn the upper body to the right slightly. Turn the toes of the left foot outward. The left fist becomes an open palm. Both palms turn to face the right and withdraw slightly. Eyes look forward (Figure 3-231).

2. 上體左轉，左腳落實，身體重心前移；右腳向前上步，停於左腳內側，兩腳平行站立，雙腳間距10

公分左右，身體稍向上伸展，重心仍在左腿。兩掌同時向上提舉，高與肩平，右掌停於身體右側，掌心向上；左掌屈肘提至體前，掌心向外。眼看右掌（圖3-232、圖3-233）。

（2）Turn the upper body to the left. Place the left foot on the ground. Shift the weight forward. The right foot steps forward and stops beside the left foot. The feet stand on parallel lines which are 10 cm apart. Stretch the body upward slightly with the weight still on the left leg. Raise both hands to shoulder level at the same time. The right hand is at the right side of the body, palm facing up; the left hand is in front of the body, elbow bent, and palm facing outward. Eyes look at the right hand (Figure 3-232, Figure 3-233).

圖3-231　　　　圖3-232　　　　圖3-233

3. 右腳以前腳掌為軸，腳跟外展，屈膝下蹲，身體重心移向右腿；上體左轉，左腳向後撤步。兩掌隨轉體向左平捋至體前，右掌高與肩平，左掌停於右肘內側，兩掌心斜相對。眼看右掌（圖3–234、圖3–235）。

（3）Pivoting on the ball of the foot, turn the right foot outward and bend the knee to lower the body. Shift the weight onto the right leg. Turn the upper body to the left. Following the turn of the body, pull the hands levelly to the left and stop them in front of the body, the right hand at shoulder level, the left hand by the right elbow, palm facing each other diagonally. Eyes look at the right hand (Figure 3–234, Figure 3–235).

4. 上體繼續左轉，身體重心移向左腿，右腳跟外展成橫襠步。兩掌隨轉體向左平捋，同時逐漸變掌為

圖3–234 圖3–235

拳，然後鬆腰、沉肩；左前臂外旋，左拳收於左腰間，拳心向上；右前臂外旋，滾肘下沉，右拳高與胸齊，停於體前，右臂半屈成弧形，拳心斜向內。眼看右拳（圖3-236a、圖3-236b）。

（4）Continue to turn the upper body to the left. Shift the weight onto the left leg. Turn the right foot outward to form a Side Bow Step. Following the body, pull the hands levelly to the left and turn the palms into fists. Then relax the waist and sink the shoulders. Rotate the left forearm outward and draw back the fist to the left waist, palm facing up. Rotate the right forearm outward and stop the right fist at chest level in front of the body, arm arched, and palm facing diagonally inward. Eyes look at the right hand (Figure 3-236a, Figure 3-236b).

圖3-236a　　　　　　　　圖3-236b

5. 上體右轉，身體重心移向右腿。右臂屈肘向上畫弧，右拳停於右額前，拳心向外；左拳自腰間向後穿出，拳心向後。眼看前方（圖3-237）。

（5）Turn the upper body to the right. Shift the weight onto the right leg. Bend the right arm, move the hand upward in an arc and stop it at the right front of the forehead, palm facing outward. The left hand thrusts backward from the left side of the waist, palm facing backward. Eyes look forward（Figure 3-237）.

6. 左腳尖外展，右腳尖內扣，身體重心左移，上體左轉。左拳翻轉變掌，自左向體前畫弧，掌心斜向下；右拳變掌向後、向下畫弧，掌心由後漸漸轉向前。頭隨體轉，眼看前方（圖3-238）。

（6）Turn the toes of the left foot outward and the toes of

圖3-237　　　　　　　　　　圖3-238

the right foot inward. Shift the weight to the left. Turn the upper body to the left. Change the left fist into an open palm while turning it over, and move it in an arc from the left to the front of the body, palm facing diagonally down. The right fist becomes an open palm and draws an arc backward and downward, palm turning over to face forward gradually. The head follows the body. Eyes look forward（Figure 3-238）.

7. 右腳向前進半步，停於左腳內側後方，腳前掌點地成丁步。右掌經右胯外側向前下方拓出，掌心斜向前方，高與小腹平；左掌掌指輕附於右前臂內側，掌心斜向下，拇指向內。眼看前下方（圖3-239a、圖3-239b）。

（7）The right foot moves a half step forward and stops behind

圖3-239a　　　　　　圖3-239b

the left foot, the ball of the foot on the ground to form a T–Step. The right hand moves to the lower front past the outside of the right hip, palm facing diagonally forward at lower abdomen level. The left hand attaches to the inner side of the right forearm lightly, palm facing diagonally down, thumb pointing inward. Eyes look to the lower front (Figure 3–239a, Figure 3–239b).

8. 右腳落實地面，上體向右擰轉，身體重心移於右腿，左腳輕輕提起。右掌向上、向右畫弧至身體右前方變成勾手，左掌仍附於右前臂內側並隨之轉動，然後收於右肘彎處，掌心向內。眼看右勾手（圖3–240、圖3–241）。

（8）Place the right foot on the ground. Twist the upper body to the right. Shift the weight onto the right leg. Lift the left

圖3–240　　　　　　　圖3–241

foot lightly. The right hand draws an arc upward and rightward, and stops in the right front of the body, changing into a hook (put all the fingers and the thumb together). The left hand, still attached to the inner side of the right forearm, follows the right hand, and then moves back to the right elbow, palm facing inward. Eyes look at the right hand (Figure 3–240, Figure 2–241).

9. 左腿向左側方仆出，右腿屈蹲成左仆步，上體左轉。左掌下落經腹前順左腿內側向前穿出，掌心向右。眼看左掌（圖3-242、圖3-243）。

(9) Extend the left leg to the left and bend the right leg to form a left Crouch Step. Turn the upper body to the left. The left hand falls down past the abdomen and thrusts forward along

圖3-242　　　　　　圖3-243

the inner side of the left leg, palm facing the right. Eyes look at the left hand (Figure 3–242, Figure 3–243).

【要點】

併步、轉體、撤步、平将要銜接配合,以腰為軸,兩手由平将轉為滾肘撅臂,向下沉勁。頭隨身體自然轉動。轉掌以前,兩腳伸展,內扣要和身體轉動一致,左手在身後畫弧不要太過。跟步時,要合胯屈腿,將右腳輕輕提起。下勢時,先仆出左腿,然後轉穿掌,右腿要全蹲,兩腿都要全腳著地,上體不可弓腰、低頭,過於前俯。

Key Points

The movements of placing the feet together, turning the body, stepping backward and pulling hands are coordinated smoothly. Using the waist as the axle, pull the hand first and then roll the elbows downward. Sink the energy. Turn the head naturally to follow the body. Before turning over the hands, stretch the feet and turn the foot inward while turning the body. When turning the body and moving the left hand backward, do not move it beyond the body. In the Follow up Step, draw in the hips, bend the legs, and lift the right foot gently. In the Crouch Step, extend the left leg first, and then thrust the hand, fully bending the right leg with both of the feet entirely on the ground. Do not bend the waist, lower the head or lean the upper body forward too much.

四十八、上步七星

【訣要】

騰身上步七星拳，迎面通天勇向前；
上擎下取遂機變，忽然退步轉身還；
勢成跨虎身中正，步號龍門穩下盤；
左手捋纏敵肘後，右掌直撲下丹田；
太極拳內多變端，進退起落要安詳；
拗手採纏人難見，順勁掤推敵更偏。

48. Step forward and Cross the Fists

Highlight

Skip forward and cross the fists,

aiming at the enemy's face.

Take a right chance to attack his upper or lower body.

Suddenly step backward and turn around the body.

Form the posture as if riding on a tiger;

firmly stand on the ground.

The left hand twists his elbow;

the right hand strikes his abdomen directly.

Grasp the enemy by twisting his hands,

comply the power to push him away.

So many changes in Tai Chi make the attack succeed.

1. 身體重心向前移動，上體左轉，左腳尖外展，右腳尖內扣，右腿自然蹬直，左腿前屈成左弓步。左掌向上、向前挑起，高與肩平；右臂內旋下落，勾尖向上，停於身後。眼看左掌（圖3-244）。

(1) Shift the weight forward. Turn the upper body to the left. Turn the toes of the left foot outward and the toes of the right foot inward. Extend the right leg naturally straight and bend the left leg to form a left Bow Step. Raise the left hand upward and forward to shoulder level. The right arm rotates inward, falls down and stops behind the body, the hook pointing up. Eyes look at the left hand (Figure 3–244).

圖3-244

2. 右腳向前上一步，腳前掌著地成右虛步。左掌變拳微向內收，拳心向內；右勾手變拳自後向前、向上架起，拳心向外；兩腕相交成十字拳，左拳在內，右拳在外，高與肩平，兩臂撐圓。眼看左拳（圖3-245）。

（2）The right foot takes a step forward, the ball of the foot on the ground to form an Empty Step. The left hand becomes a fist and draws back, palm facing inward. The right hand changes into a fist and pushes upward and forward, palm facing outward. The two wrists intersect to form an "X" (Cross the Fists) at shoulder level, the left fist on the inside and the right fist on the outside, arms arched. Eyes look at the left hand (Figure 3–245).

【要點】

起身前，隨上體左轉，左腳尖儘量外擺，右腳尖

圖3-245

儘量內扣。起身時，合胯、提腿，上步要輕勻平穩，
定式時肩胯要鬆沉。

Key Points

When turning the upper body to the left, turn the toes of
the left foot outward and the toes of the right foot inward as much
as possible. Draw in the hips, lift the leg up and step forward
lightly and stably. When the posture is settled, sink the hips
and shoulders.

四十九、結印歸元

1. 右腳內扣，身體重心移向右腿，左腳輕提收至
右腳左側平行站立。同時，兩拳變掌自上向下、向兩
側畫立圓到頭頂上方。眼看正前方。兩掌中指相對，
從頭頂上方經面部、腹部向下按至小腹臍下，雙腿微
屈（圖3-246）。

49. Closing

（1）Turn the toes of the right foot inward. Shift the weight
onto the right leg. Lift the left foot lightly and move it close and
parallel to the right foot. Meanwhile, both hands turn into open
palms and draw vertical circles downward and to either side,
until they are over the head, the middle fingers pointing at
each other. Eyes look forward. Then move the hands past the
face and the chest, and press them down in front of the lower

abdomen. Legs bend slightly (Figure 3–246).

2. 兩掌向兩側分開，轉掌心向下，手指向前；同時，兩掌移至褲縫處（圖3–247）。

（2）Separate the hands apart and turn the palms over to face down, fingers pointing forward. Meanwhile, move the hands by the outside of the thighs (Figure 3–247).

3. 挺胸收腹，兩臂伸直，兩掌根向身後推進（圖3–248）。

（3）Stretch chest and draw in abdomen. Extend the arms straight. Push the bases of the hands backward (Figure 3–248).

4. 上體向前下方俯身塌腰90°，雙臂向後上方翹

圖3–246 　　　　圖3–247 　　　　圖3–248

起，保持挺胸姿勢，頭背成一水平直線（圖3-249a、3-249b）。

（4）Bend the body and the waist to 90°. Lift the arms and hands behind the body. Keep the chest stretched. The head and the back are at the same level, which is parallel to the ground（Figure 3-249a, Figure 3-249b）.

5. 保持俯身姿勢，兩臂向左右分開，與背成一直線，兩掌心均朝天（圖3-250）。

（5）With the waist bent, separate both hands apart to form a straight line with the back, palms facing upward（Figure 3-250）.

6. 上體後坐直立；同時，屈膝下蹲成馬步。兩臂

圖3-249a   圖3-249b

保持原狀，兩掌心隨勢轉向前方（圖3–251）。

（6）Straighten the upper body and move it backward. Meanwhile, bend the knees and lower the body, and turn the palms to face forward (Figure 3–251).

7. 略含胸，鬆肩，屈肘，雙掌自兩側向小腹處下落，隨勢雙掌轉掌心向內成抱球狀，保持屈膝狀態

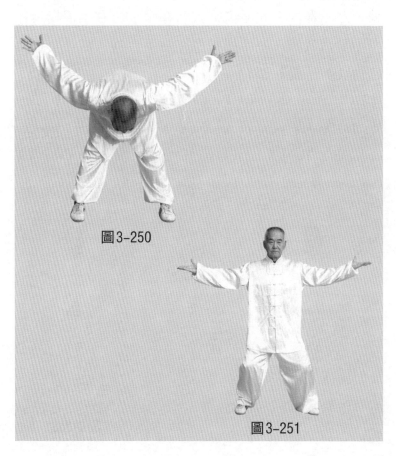

圖3–250

圖3–251

（圖3-252）。

（7）Draw the chest in slightly. Relax the shoulders and bend the elbows to move the hands down to abdomen, palms facing inward as if holding a ball. The knees are still bent at this moment（Figure 3-252）.

8. 身體緩緩直立；同時，兩掌虎口相叉，右手在外，左手在內，左手勞宮穴對在臍上，右手拇指壓在左手勞宮穴處，左手拇指壓在右手合谷穴處（女性與之相反）（圖3-253）。

（8）Stand up slowly. Put the hands together, with the Tiger Mouths（middle point of the thumb and index finger）touching each other. The left hand is on the inside, it's Lao Gong Xue（an acupunctural point located on the palm of a hand, the

圖3-252　　　　　　　圖3-253

point at which the middle finger points while the hand forms a fist) on the navel and the thumb touching the "He Gu Xue" (an acupunctural point located on the back of a hand, between the Tiger Mouth and the wrist) of the right hand. The right hand is on the outside, thumb pressing the Lao Gong Xue of the left hand (For a female, switch the position of the left hand with the right hand) (Figure 3–253).

9. 雙掌按順時針方向摩腹36圈,再按逆時針方向摩腹24圈,然後靜立兩分鐘(圖3–254)。

(9) Keep above posture. Massage the abdomen 36 times clockwise with both hands, and 24 times counterclockwise. Then close the eyes and stand still for 2 minutes (Figure 3–254).

圖3–254

10. 收功。兩掌向左右分開，沿褲縫下垂於身體兩側。同時，左腳向右腳靠攏（圖3-255）。

(10) Separate the hands to the opposite sides and hang them down by the outside of the thighs. Move the left foot close to the right foot. The routine is finished (Figure 3-255).

圖3-255

四十八式養生太極拳二人對練

Two Person Exercises of 48 Form Tai Chi
for Health Maintenance and Improvement

一、對練推手

太極拳推手可以分成掤、擠、捋、按四個基本動作。這四個動作是連續、完整的。太極拳推手之鍛鍊要達到：有力似無力，無力似有力。這樣，全身各處肌肉定會放鬆，使全身成為整體力量，而且能很好地加以發揮並應用在推手之中。

Section 1　Two-Person Push

The basic movements which are used in Tai Chi to push each other are Peng, Ji, Lǚ, An. During the exercises, the four movements are seamless and united as one. Relax the entire body so that it appears soft but is strong with unnoticed power.

1. 單人練習法

（1）預備式。此式要求與太極拳預備式相同（圖4-1）。

1. Solo Exercises

（1）Preparing. Follow（Figure 4-1）.

（2）接上式，半面向左轉，左足尖外擺寸許（斜方），右足尖內扣寸許（要直向前方）。頭正，身直，目正視（圖4-2）。

（2）Turn the head to the left. Swing the toes of the left foot outward about 3-4cm, toes pointing to the left front. Swing the toes of the right foot inward about 3-4cm, toes pointing forward. Keep the head and body straight. Eyes look straight to the front（Figure 4-2）.

【掤】

（1）接上式，左足不動，右足直向前一步平

圖4-1　　　　　　　　　　圖4-2

落，兩足成丁八步（尾閭中正）。同時，兩手反轉從胸前而出，右手在前，高與頭平，手心向內，形如抱球；左手心向外，高與右肘平，距離肩寬，形如推球。「手足合」，「肩胯合」，肘膝相對，兩手五指鬆弛。注意挺頸，身直，目視兩手中間（圖4-3）。

Peng（Push with the Forearm）

(1) Keep the left foot unchanged. The right foot takes a step forward. The two feet form a「\ /」shape. Meanwhile, push both hands forward. The right hand is ahead, at head level, palm facing inward, as if holding a ball. The left hand is facing outward, the same level as the right elbow, as if pushing a ball. The hands are coordinated with the feet, as the shoulders are with the hips. The elbows are aligned with the knees. Fingers are relaxed. Keep the neck and body straight. Eyes look between the hands (Figure 4–3).

(2) 接上式，胯向左轉，右膝徐徐轉動向前，至足尖一寸內，左膝微屈（似挺非挺）。同時，兩臂轉動向前，右手內旋，小指內擰，斜向上舒，腕與頭平；左手小指外擰，手心要空，形如向前拓球（似著非著，似離非離）。右足主力，左足吸力。頭正，身直，目視兩手中間（圖4-4）。

(2) Turn the hips to the left. Move the right knee forward

slowly about 3–4cm. Bend the left knee slightly. Meanwhile, rotate both arms forward. The right hand turns inward and the little finger points up diagonally, the wrist at head level. The left hand turns outward, palm arched as if pushing a ball forward. Deliver the force from the left foot to the right. Keep the head and body straight. Eyes look between the hands (Figure 4–4).

【擠】

（1）接上式，兩足原地不動，胯向右轉，左胯下沉，右胯回吸。右手臂原式徐徐下沉，左手翻轉至右臂根，手心斜向上，形如抱球（臂成圓弧形）。頭頂，身直，目視兩手中間（圖4-5）。

圖4-3　　　　圖4-4　　　　圖4-5

Ji (Push with the Upper Forearm)

（1）Keep both feet unchanged. Twist the hips to the right. Sink the left hip and suck back the right hip. Keep the form and lower the right hand and arm heavily and slowly. Turn the left hand over beside the right armpit, palm facing up diagonally as if holding a ball. Draw the head up. Keep the body straight. Eyes look between the hands（Figure 4-5）.

（2）接上式，胯向右轉正。同時，左手背撐右臂，右肱自然向前「擠」，右手翻轉扶左肘，兩小臂向前與肩平，形如抱球。右膝在足尖一寸內，左膝微屈，似挺非挺。右足主力，左足吸力（小腹、膝蓋、足尖列成直線）。頭頂，身直，目正視（圖4-6）。

（2）Twist the hips back. Meanwhile, the back of the left hand pushes the right arm; the right forearm pushes forward. The right hand turns over to touch the left elbow. Push both forearms forward at shoulder level as if holding a ball with the arms. Twist the right knee inward slightly. Bend the left knee slightly without being noticed. Deliver the force from the left foot to the right. Keep the head and body straight. Eyes look straight forward（Figure 4-6）.

【捋】

（1）接上式，右胯向下沉，兩手隨胯而動，左手翻轉，小指內擰，斜向上舒（成弧形），腕與頭平；右手翻轉斜向下指，與胯平，小指向上，手臂鬆弛，兩肘距離4～5寸。右足主力，左足吸力。頭正，身直，目視兩手中間（圖4-7）。

Lǚ(Pull)

（1）Sink the right hip. Both hands follow the hip. The left hand turns over, the little finger moves inward and points up diagonally, palm arched, wrist at head level. The right hand turns over by the hip, the little finger pointing up and the rest of the fingers pointing down diagonally. Relax the hands, with the elbows 20cm apart. The left foot gathers the power and the right foot uses it. Keep the head and body straight. Eyes look

圖4-6 　　　　　　圖4-7

between the hands（Figure 4–7）.

（2）接上式，屈膝坐身，胯向左轉，重心隨轉隨移至左足。同時，左手臂圓轉至左前方，手心向外，食指高與頭平；右手臂圓轉至正前方，手心向內，高與左手同。兩肘距離肩寬，兩臂成圓弧形。左足主力，右足吸力。頭頂，身直，目正視（圖4-8）。

（2）Bend the legs and lower the body. Turn the hips to the left and shift the weight onto the left foot. Meanwhile, move the left hand to the left front, palm facing outward, the index finger at head level. Move the right hand in front of the forehead to the same height as the left hand, palm facing in. The elbows are apart with shoulder width, both arms are arched. The right foot gathers the power and the left foot uses it. Keep the head and body straight. Eyes look straight forward（Figure 4-8）.

【按】

（1）接上式，左胯下沉，「空胸緊背」，兩手隨胯而動，翻轉下按，兩肘自然上提，高與胸平，中指對，兩肱圓。頭頂，身直，目視兩手中間（圖4-9）。

An（Push with Both Hands）

（1）Sink the left hip. Stretch the back and tuck the chest

in slightly. Both hands follow the hip to push down and turn over. Lift both elbows up to chest level. Both middle fingers are pointing at each other. Both arms are arched. Keep the head and body straight. Eyes look between the hands (Figure 4–9).

（2）接上式，胯向右轉，重心移至右足，右膝在足面一寸內，左膝微屈，似挺非挺。同時，兩手向前撐至右前方，形如扶球。注意鬆展。右手食指尖與頭平，左手大拇指對右肘，距離肩寬。頭頂，身直，目視兩手中間（圖4-10）。

（2）Turn the hips to the right, and shift the weight onto the right foot. Push the right knee inward slightly. Bend the left knee slightly. Meanwhile, push both hands to the right front as if supporting a ball. The right index fingertip is at head level.

圖4-8   圖4-9

The left thumb is pointing at the right elbow, shoulder width apart. Keep the head and body straight. Eyes look between the hands (Figure 4–10).

（3）接上式，屈膝坐身，右胯下沉。同時，兩手翻轉（成圓弧形），右手心向內，左手心向外，與推手第三動作相同（圖4-11）。

（3）Bend the knee and lower the body. Sink the right hip. Meanwhile, both hands turn over, arched, the right palm facing inward, the left palm facing outward (Figure 4–11).

（4）接上式，左足不動，右足提起至左足跟並落實。同時，兩手翻轉至胸前，手心均向下徐徐下垂，

圖4-10　　　　圖4-11　　　　圖4-12

繼續半面向右轉。兩足與預備式相同（圖4-12）。

(4) Keep the left foot unchanged. Lift the right foot and place it close to the left foot. Meanwhile, bring both hands in front of the chest, palms facing down. Both hands fall down slowly and turn the body 45° to the right. The feet assume the position of「Preparing」(Figure 4-12).

2. 雙人練習法（演練者：陳杰、李建軍）

(1)預備式

①甲（黑衣）、乙（白衣）二人相對而立，距離兩步。姿勢與單人操練預備式相同（如圖4-1）。

2. Two Person Exercises

(1) Preparing

a. Person A (the one wearing black clothes) and Person B (the one wearing white clothes) stand up, facing each other, about 1m apart. Postures are the same as Preparing in the Solo Exercises (as Figure 4-1).

②甲乙二人原式各半面向左轉（約45°）。姿勢與單人操練預備式相同（如圖4-2）。

b. Both Person A and Person B turn to the left about 45°. Postures are the same as ones used in Prepare in Solo Exercises (as Figure 4-2).

（2）出手式

甲、乙左足原地不動，各以右足向前一步，甲、乙兩足內側相對，距離三四寸（各為丁八步）。手隨足動，兩手反轉從胸前而出，甲、乙之右手背相黏，五指上舒，手心向內，中指與頭平；甲、乙之左手各扶對方之右肘，兩肱圓。左足主力，右足吸力。頭正，身直，尾閭中正，目視兩手中間（圖4-13）。

（2）Start

Both people keep their left foot unchanged and take a step forward with their right foot. The inner side of Person A's right foot faces the inner side of Person B's right foot, 15cm apart. Their hands follow the feet to push forward from the chest, the back of their right hands touching, fingers stretched, palms facing inward, middle fingers at head level. Person A's left

圖4-13

hand attaches itself to Person B's right elbow, so does Person B to Person A. The arms are arched. For both: the right foot gathers the power and the left uses it. Keep the head and body straight. Eyes look between the hands (Figure 4-13).

(3)乙掤甲；甲順乙，掤勁變捋

①接上式，乙左胯沉，右胯徐徐轉動向前，右膝屈，左膝微屈，似挺非挺。同時，兩臂旋轉，右手小指內擰，斜向上舒（右小臂外側為掤），左臂弧形，手心斜向前，兩肘與肩平。頭正，身直，目視兩手中間（圖4-14）。

(3) Person B Peng Person A; Person A follows Person B; Person B switches Peng to Lǚ

a. Person B: Sink the left hip and move the right hip forward slowly. Bend both knees slightly. Meanwhile, rotate both arms, the right little finger stretched up diagonally (deliver the power to the outside of the right forearm, which is called Peng). The left arm is arched, palm facing forward diagonally. The elbows are at shoulder level. Keep the head and body straight. Eyes look between the hands (Figure 4-14).

②甲同時（隨乙動）右胯回吸，兩手順乙之右臂轉動，右手黏乙右手，隨轉動反轉手心向外，左手小

指內撐，以小臂外側将乙之右臂，左肘對右膝。右足
吸力，左足主力。頭正，身直，尾閭中正，目視兩手
中間（圖4-14）。

b. Person A: At the same time, draw the right hip in. The
hands follow Person B's right arm. The right hand attaches to
Person B's right hand and the palm turns to face outward. The
little finger of the left hand rotates inward, and the outer flank
of his left arm attaches to and pulls Person B's right arm. The
left elbow is aligned with his right knee. The right foot gathers
the power and the left foot uses the power. Keep the head and
body straight. Eyes look between the hands (Figure 4–14).

（4）乙順甲，捋勁變擠；甲順乙，擠勁變按

①接上式，乙左胯沉，右胯吸（胯向右轉）。手
隨胯動，右臂下沉，左手反轉至右臂根，手心斜向
上，手背撑動右臂，左臂自然向前擠。左手順甲之
意，將甲之右手領至左肘，手心向內，（不停）反轉
下鬆。右足主力，左足似蹬非蹬。頭頂，身直，目正
視（圖4-15）。

（4）Person B follows Person A and switches Lǔ to Ji;
Person A follows Person B and switches Ji to An

a. Person B: Sink the left hip and turn the right hip to the
right. Sink the right arm and move the left hand by the right

armpit, palm facing up diagonally. The left hand rubs and pushes the right arm forward. Then the left hand pulls Person A's right hand, palm facing inward. The right foot uses the power; left foot pushes the ground. Keep the head and body straight. Eyes look straight forward（Figure 4-15）.

②甲同時左胯回吸轉正，兩手隨胯而動，空胸緊背。兩手徐徐反轉下按（兩肘自然上提），手心斜向前，兩肱圓，右手按乙之左肘，左手按乙之左手背。左足主力，右足吸力。頭頂，身直，目視兩手中間（圖4-15）。

b. Person A: At the same time, turn the left hip and body to face the front. Both hands move with the hip. Stretch the back and draw the chest in. Push both hands down slowly with

圖4-14　　　　圖4-15

elbows up naturally, palms facing forward diagonally. Arms are arched. The right hand pushes Person B's left elbow. The left hand presses Person B's back of the left hand. The right foot gathers the power and the left foot uses it. Keep the head and body straight. Eyes look between the hands (Figure 4–15).

③接上式，甲左胯回吸，右胯向前，兩手攬乙之左臂，斜向上舒，右手心扶乙之左肘，左手扶乙之左手背。右足主力，左足吸力。頭頂，身直，目視兩手中間（圖4-16）。

c. Person A: Draw back the left hip and push the right hip forward. Both hands pull Person B's left arm upward diagonally. The right hand sticks to Person B's left elbow and left hand sticks to the back of Person B's left hand. The right foot gathers the power and the left uses the power. Keep the head and body straight. Eyes look between the hands (Figure 4–16).

④乙同時屈膝坐身，胯向右轉，兩手反轉。左手小指內撐領甲之兩手，斜向上舒，右手小指向上（外撐）斜向下指。左足主力，右足吸力。頭正，身直，目視兩手中間（圖4-16）。

d. Person B: Bend the knees and lower the body. Turn the hip to the right, and turn both hands over. Rotate the left hand

48式養生太極拳

inward to lead Person A's hands upward diagonally. Rotate the right hand outward so that the side of the little finger faces up and the finger points down diagonally. The right foot gathers the power and the left uses the power. Keep the head and body straight. Eyes look between the hands (Figure 4–16).

（5）甲按變掤；乙順甲，掤變捋

①接上式，甲右胯沉，左胯轉動向前，右膝屈，左膝微屈（似挺非挺）。同時，兩臂旋轉，左手小指內擰，斜向上舒（左小臂外側為掤），右臂成弧形，手心斜向前，肘與臂平。頭正，身直，目視兩手中間（圖4–17）。

（5）Person A switches An to Peng; Person B follows Person A and switches Peng to Lǔ

圖4–16　　　　　　圖4–17

a. Person A: Sink the right hip and move the left hip forward slowly; bend the right knee and the left knee slightly. Meanwhile, rotate both arms, the left little finger stretched up diagonally (deliver the power to the outside of the right forearm, which is called Peng). The right arm is arched, palm facing forward diagonally. The elbows are at shoulder level. Keep the head and body straight. Eyes look between the hands (Figure 4-17).

②乙同時（隨甲動）左胯回吸，兩手順甲左臂轉動，左手背黏甲左手斜向上領（要鬆展），右小指內撑，以小臂內側轉動捋甲之左臂。右肘對右膝。左足主力，右足吸力。頭正，身直，目視兩手中間（圖4-17）。

b. Person B: At the same time, draw the left hip in. Both hands follow Person A's left arm. The left hand sticks to Person A's left hand, and leads it upward diagonally. The little finger of the right hand rotates inward. The inter flank of the right arm sticks to and pulls Person A's left arm. The right elbow is aligned with the right knee. The right foot gathers the power and the left foot uses the power. Keep the head and body straight. Eyes look between the hands (Figure 4-17).

（6）甲順乙，将變擠；乙順甲，擠變按

①接上式，甲右胯沉，左胯吸（胯向左轉），手隨胯動。左臂下沉，右手反轉至左肩根，手心斜向上，右手背撐動左臂，右臂自然向前擠。左手順乙之意，將乙之左手領至右肘，手心向內（不停）反轉下鬆。右足主力，左足似蹬非蹬。頭頂，身直，目正視（圖4-18）。

（6）Person A follows Person B and switches Lǚ to Ji; Person B follows Person A and switches Ji to An

a. Person A: Sink the right hip and turn the left hip to the left. Sink the left arm and move the right hand by the left armpit, palm facing up diagonally. The right hand rubs and pushes the left arm forward. Then the left hand pulls Person B's left hand, palm facing inward. The right foot uses the power; left

圖4-18

foot pushes the ground. Keep the head and body straight. Eyes look straight forward（Figure 4–18）.

②乙同時右胯回吸轉正，兩手隨胯而動。空胸緊背，兩手徐徐反轉下按（兩肘自然上提），手心斜向前，兩肱圓，左手按甲之右手背。左足主力，右足吸力。頭正，身直，目視兩手中間（圖4–18）。

b. Person B: At the same time, turn the right hip and body to face front. Both hands move with the hip. Stretch the back and draw the chest in. Push both hands down slowly with elbows naturally up, palms facing forward diagonally. Arms are arched. The left hand presses against the back of Person A's right hand. The right foot gathers the power and the left foot uses the power. Keep the head and body straight. Eyes look between the hands（Figure 4–18）.

③接上式，乙右胯回吸，左胯向前，兩手攙甲之右臂，斜向上舒，左手扶甲之右肘，右手扶甲右手背。右足主力，左膝微屈，似挺非挺。頭正，身直，目視兩手中間（圖4–19）。

c. Person B: Draw back the right hip and push the left hip forward. Both hands pull Person A's right arm upward diagonally; the left hand sticks to Person A's right elbow, the right hand sticks to the back of Person A's right hand. The left knee bends slightly and the right foot uses the power. Keep the head and body straight. Eyes look between the hands (Figure 4-19).

④甲同時屈膝坐身，胯向左轉，兩手反轉。右手小指內擰，領乙之兩手斜向上舒；左手小指向外擰，小指向上，斜向下指。左足主力，右足吸力。頭正，身直，目視兩手中間（圖4-19）。

d. Person A: At the same time, bend the knees and lower the body. Turn the hip to the left, and turn both hands over. Rotate the right little finger inward to lead Person B's hands upward diagonally. Rotate the left hand outward so that the side of the little finger faces up and the finger points down diagonally. The right foot gathers the power and the left foot uses the pow-

圖4-19

er. Keep the head and body straight. Eyes look between the hands (Figure 4-19).

（7）乙再變掤；甲順乙，掤變捋

如上圖解，循環不已。

（7）Person B changes to Peng; Person A follows Person B and switches Peng to Lǚ

Repeat above movements again and again.

①甲乙練習終止時，與第一圖解說明相同。

②甲乙各以右足撤至左足，同時各以兩手反轉經胸前下鬆，半面向右，轉歸原收式。

When the exercises are finished, both withdraw their right foot back to the left foot. Hands fall down in front of the chest. Postures are the same as Preparing (as Figure 4-1).

二、拓三節

拓三節和大纏主要以纏手動作為基礎（圖4-20～圖4-23）。

Section 2 Exercises on the Three Sections of the Upper Limbs (Hands, Elbows and Shoulders)

Exercises on the three sections of the upper limbs and the twisted force, based on the hand twisting (Figure 4-20 ～ Figure 4–23）.

【要領】

拓手時雙方手心均向下。

Key Points

Both hands of A and B face down.

圖4–20

圖4–21

圖4–22

圖4–23

（一）拓梢節

1. 預備式

甲、乙對面立正站立，相距兩步（圖4-24）。

1. Exercises of the End Section（Hands）

（1）Preparing

Person A（the one wearing black clothes in Figure 4-24）and Person B（the one wearing white clothes in Figure 4-24）stand up and face each other, 90-100cm apart（Figure 4-24）.

2. 起　式

甲、乙同時於腹前捧手至胸前，中指相對，掌心向上（圖4-25）。

（2）Start

Both Person A and Person B move their hands from their

圖4-24　　　　　　圖4-25

abdomen to their chest, palms facing up, the right and left middle fingers pointing at each other (Figure 4-25).

3. 拓 手

甲右腳上一步，兩手臂內旋向乙方胸前推出；乙左腳退一步，兩手臂內旋以手掌拓甲兩腕背側（圖4-26）。

(3) Exercising the hands

Person A's right foot takes a step forward and pushes Person B's chest. Person B's left foot takes a step backward and pushes Person A's wrists (Figure 4-26).

4. 內 纏

（1）乙做內纏，甲亦隨乙內纏一圈；甲被拓至

圖4-26

兩側外方時，以兩手腕內側繞至乙手腕外側上方（圖4-27）。

（2）甲做內纏，乙亦隨甲內纏一圈；乙被拓至兩側外方時，以兩手腕內側繞至甲手腕外側上方（圖4-28、圖4-29）。

（4）Twist Inward

a. Person B twists inward; Person A follows. When Person A's arms are moved to the sides of his body, Person A moves his wrists from the inner side of Person B's wrist to the outside of the Person B's wrists (Figure 4-27).

b. Person A twists inward; Person B follows. When Person B's arms are moved to the sides of his body, Person B moves his wrists from the inner side of Person A's wrists to the outside of the Person A's wrists (Figure 4-28, Figure 4-29).

圖4-27　　　　　　　圖4-28

【要領】

纏手一方重心前移，被纏一方重心後坐。內纏動作要反覆練習。

Key Points

The person who leads shifts the weight forward; the other person shifts the weight backward. Practice repeatedly.

5. 外　纏

（1）甲做外纏，乙亦隨甲外纏一圈；乙被拓至內側時，以兩手腕外側繞至甲兩手腕內側上方（圖4-30）。

（2）甲乙動作互換，反覆練習。

（5）Twist Outward

a. Person A twists outward; Person B follows. When Per-

圖4-29　　　　　　圖4-30

son B's arms are moved by the front of his body, Person B moves the wrists from the outside of Person A's wrists to the inner side of the Person A's wrists (Figure 4–30).

b. Person A and Person B exchange positions and practice repeatedly.

6.左　纏

（1）甲拓乙手腕做左纏，乙亦隨甲左纏而做本身的右纏（圖4–31、圖4–32）。

（2）乙被纏至左側時，雙手經甲兩腕右側繞至甲兩腕上方，做右纏（圖4–33）。

（6）Twist Leftward

a. Person A's wrist sticks to Person B's wrist and pushes it to the left. Person B follows Person A and moves the same way

圖4–31　　　　　　　　　圖4–32

in an opposite direction (Figure 4–31, Figure 4–32).

b. When Person B's hands reach the left side of his body, they move along the right side of Person A's wrists, move onto the wrists, and repeat above movement in an opposite direction (Figure 4–33).

【要領】

纏手一方重心前移，被纏一方重心後移。

Key Points

The person who leads shifts the weight forward; the other person shifts the weight backward.

7. 右　纏

甲乙互換，動作與左纏相同，唯方向相反。

圖4-33

（7）Twist Rightward

Person A and Person B exchange positions and repeat Twist Leftward.

（二）拓中節

1. 預備式

同拓梢節之預備式。

2. Exercises on the Middle Section（Elbows）

（1）Preparing

Same as the Preparing of Exercises of the End Section（Hands）

2. 起　式

同拓梢節之起式。

（2）Start

Same as the Start of Exercises of the End Section（Hands）

3. 拓　肘

甲右腳上一步，兩手臂內旋向乙方胸前推出；乙左腳退一步，兩手臂內旋以手掌拓甲兩肘（圖4-34）。

（3）Exercising elbows

Person A takes a step forward and pushes Person B's chest

with both hands. Person B takes a step backward and pushes Person A's elbows with both hands (Figure 4–34).

4. 內　纏

乙做內纏，甲亦隨乙內纏一圈；甲被拓至兩側外方時，以兩手腕內側繞至乙肘部外側上方（圖4-35）。甲乙互換動作，反覆練習。

(4) Twist Inward

Person B twists inward; Person A follows. When Person A's arms are moved to the sides of his body, Person A moves his wrists from the inner side of Person B's elbow to the outside of the Person B's elbow (Figure 4–35). Person A and Person B exchange positions and practice repeatedly.

圖4-34　　　　　　　圖4-35

5. 外　纏

甲做外纏，乙亦隨甲外纏一圈；乙被拓至胸前內側時，從兩手腕外側繞至甲肘部上方（圖4-36）。甲乙互換動作，反覆練習。

（5）Twist Outward

Person A twists outward; Person B follows. When Person B's arms are moved to the front of the chest, Person B moves his wrists from the outsides of Person A's elbows to the inner sides of the Person A's elbows (Figure 4–36). Person A and Person B exchange positions and practice repeatedly.

6. 左　纏

（1）乙拓甲兩肘部做左纏，甲亦隨乙左纏而做本身的右纏（圖4-37、圖4-38）。

圖4-36　　　　　圖4-37

（2）甲被纏至左側時，雙手經乙兩肘部右側繞至乙兩肘上方，做右纏（圖4-39）。

（6）Twist Leftward

a. Person B's wrist sticks to Person A's elbow and pushes it to the left. Person A follows Person B and moves the same way in an opposite direction (Figure 4–37, Figure 4–38).

b. When Person A reaches the left side of his body, both hands along Person B's right side of the elbow, move onto the Person B's elbows and repeat above movement in an opposite direction (Figure 4–39).

【要領】

纏手中手心均向下，纏手時重心向前，被纏時重心向後。甲乙互換動作，反覆練習。

圖4-38　　　　　　　圖4-39

Key Points

Both people's hands face down. The person who leads shifts the weight forward; the other person shifts the weight backward. Person A and Person B exchange positions and practice repeatedly.

7. 右　纏

甲乙互換，動作與左纏相同，唯方向相反。

(7) Twist Rightward

Person A and Person B exchange positions and repeat Twist Leftward.

(三) 拓根節

1. 預備式

同拓梢節之預備式。

3. Exercises on the Root Section (Shoulders)

(1) Preparing

Same as Preparing for Exercises of the End Section (Hands).

2. 起　式

同拓梢節之起式。

(2) Start

Same as Start for Exercises of the End Section (Hands).

3. 白鶴亮翅

甲以兩手臂內旋，手心向外，中指相對，拓乙胸部，重心前移。乙兩手臂內旋，手心向兩側，手背相貼，小指側向上，屈臂，重心後移，化開甲方進攻（圖4-40）。

乙化開甲方進攻，即以兩掌拓甲胸部，動作同前甲；甲方化解動作同前動之乙（圖4-41）。

甲乙互換動作，反覆練習。

(3) Refer to White Crane Spreads Wings.

Person A rotates both arms inward, palms facing forward, his right middle fingers pointing at the left, and vice versa. Per-

圖4-40　　　　圖4-41

son A pushes Person B's chest and shifts the weight forward. Person B rotates both arms inward, palms facing outward, the backs of the hands together, the side of little fingers facing up, arms bent. Person B shifts the weight backward to guide Person A's force away (Figure 4-40) and pushes Person A's chest the same way with Person A did to Person B. Person A moves the same way to lead Person B's force away (Figure 4-41).

Person A and Person B exchange positions and Practice repeatedly.

4. 內　纏

（1）甲兩手拇指向上，以虎口拓乙之肩關節，重心前移（圖4-42）。

（2）乙兩手內纏，拇指向上，以虎口拓甲之肩

圖4-42

48式養生太極拳

關節，重心前移（圖4-43）。

(4) Twist Inward

a. Person A: Both thumbs point up. Tiger Mouths (the middle point of the thumb and index finger) stick to Person B's shoulders. Shift the weight forward (Figure 4-42).

b. Person B: Twist both hands inward, thumbs pointing up. Tiger Mouths stick to Person A's shoulders. Shift the weight forward (Figure 4-43).

【要領】

隨對方進攻重心略後移，以化解對方之力。

Key Points

When the enemy attacks you, move backward to lead his force away.

圖4-43

5.外　纏

（1）甲兩臂內旋，小指側向上，以虎口拓乙之肩關節，重心前移；乙重心略後移，兩手臂內旋、外纏至甲方肩部，小指側向上（圖4-44）。

（2）乙拓甲之肩關節，重心略前移；甲之重心略後移，化開乙方之力，兩手臂成內旋，小指側向上，外纏至乙方肩部（圖4-45）。

甲乙互換動作，反覆練習。

（5）Twist Outward

a. Person A rotates both arms inward, the side of little fingers facing up. Tiger Mouths stick to Person B's shoulders. Person A shifts the weight forward. Person B shifts the weight backward. Person B rotates the arms inward and twists the hand to catch Person A's shoulders, the side of his little fingers fac-

圖4-44　　　　　圖4-45

ing up (Figure 4–44).

b. Person B rubs Person A's shoulder and shifts the weight forward slightly. Person A shifts the weight backward slightly and guides away Person B's force. Person A rotates both arms inward and twists the hands to catch Person B's shoulders, the side of his little fingers facing up (Figure 4–45).

Person A and Person B exchange positions and repeat the above movements.

6. 大　纏

（1）甲左臂內旋，屈肘，手心向外，拇指向下，扶乙右小臂；右臂內旋，拇指向下，前伸，向左轉體纏乙肋部（圖4-46）。

（2）乙左臂內旋，拇指向下，屈肘，以左掌扶

圖4-46

甲右臂化開甲方進攻（圖4-47），隨即以右臂內旋、
屈肘內纏化開甲方左臂之進攻。同時，左臂內旋、前
伸，纏甲方肋部（圖4-48）。體略右轉。

(6)Big Twist

a. Person A rotates his left arm inward and bends the elbow, palm facing outward, thumb pointing down. Person A's
left hand sticks to Person B's right forearm. Person A rotates
his right arm inward, thumb pointing down, and turns his body
to the left to strike Person B's ribs (Figure 4-46).

b. Person B rotates his left arm inward, thumb pointing
down, and bends the elbow. The left hand sticks to Person A's
right arm to lead his attack away (Figure 4-47). Person B's
right arm rotates inward and bends the elbow to lead Person A's
left arm's attack away. Person B's left arm rotates and twists for-

圖4-47　　　　　　圖4-48

ward to attack Person A's ribs (Figure 4–48). Person B turns to the right slightly.

【要領】

一側化解的同時對側進攻。轉體與動作協調配合。

Key Points

Use one arm to lead the enemy away, and use the other to attack him. The body is coordinated with the movement.

7. 收 式

（1）甲兩手心相對，拇指向上，肘（肘略屈）托乙肘部，重心略後移；乙手心向下，扶甲之兩小臂內上方，臂略屈。

（2）雙方前腳後撤、併步，兩手臂經腹前外展，向兩側上方提起，畫弧至頭前。掌心向外，中指相對，經面前屈臂下落至腹前（圖4–49）。恢復立正姿勢。

(7) Closing

a. Both of Person A's hands face each other, thumbs pointing up, elbows bent slightly as he holds Person B's elbows. Person A shifts the weight backward slightly. Person B's hands face down and stick to Person A's forearms, arms bent slightly.

b. Both Person A's and Person B's front foot draws back to

the other foot. Both move hands outward to the front of the abdomen, then lift and stop them in front of the head, palms facing outward, the right and left middle fingers pointing at each
other. Move the hands past the face to the abdomen (Figure 4-
49), then back to the posture of Preparing.

圖4-49

彩色圖解太極武術

養生保健 古今養生保健法 強身健體增加身體免疫力

健康加油站

健康加油站

武術武道技術

截拳道入門

體育教材

運動精進叢書

快樂健美站

歡迎至本公司購買書籍

建議路線

1. 搭乘捷運、公車

　　淡水線石牌站下車，由石牌捷運站2號出口出站(出站後靠右邊)，沿著捷運高架往台北方向走(往明德站方向)，其街名為西安街，約走100公尺(勿超過紅綠燈)，由西安街一段293巷進來(巷口有一公車站牌，站名為自強街口)，本公司位於致遠公園對面。搭公車者請於石牌站(石牌派出所)下車，走進自強街，遇致遠路口左轉，右手邊第一條巷子即為本社位置。

2. 自行開車或騎車

　　由承德路接石牌路，看到陽信銀行右轉，此條即為致遠一路二段，在遇到自強街(紅綠燈)前的巷子(致遠公園)左轉，即可看到本公司招牌。

國家圖書館出版品預行編目資料

48式養生太極拳 ／ 苗樹林 編著
——初版，——臺北市，大展，2015〔民104 .10〕
面；21公分 ——（中英文對照武學；8）
ISBN 978－986－346－088－6（平裝；附影音光碟）

1.太極拳 2.養生
528.972 104015542

48 式養生太極拳 附VCD

編 著／苗樹林
責任編輯／王躍平 張東黎
發 行 人／蔡森明
出 版 者／大展出版社有限公司
社 址／台北市北投區（石牌）致遠一路2段12巷1號
電 話／（02）28236031・28236033・28233123
傳 眞／（02）28272069
郵政劃撥／01669551
網 址／www.dah-jaan.com.tw
E - mail ／service@dah-jaan.com.tw
登 記 證／局版臺業字第2171號
承 印 者／傳興印刷有限公司
裝 訂／眾友企業公司
排 版 者／弘益電腦排版有限公司
授 權 者／山西科學技術出版社
初版1刷／2015年（民104年）10月

定 價／400元

●本書若有破損、缺頁請寄回本社更換●